Vere Foster

Vere Foster

English Gentleman,
Irish Champion
1819–1900

BRENDAN COLGAN

FOUNTAIN PUBLISHING
BELFAST

Published 2001
by Fountain Publishing

© 2001 Fountain Publishing

ISBN 0-9525565-6-1

Printed by Creative Print and Design Group
Design by Dunbar Design

CONTENTS

ACKNOWLEDGEMENTS

In the production of this book, the publishers would like to thank a number of individuals for their assistance. These include Mrs Colette Colgan, Father Patrick Colgan, Mr John Colgan, Mrs Mary Kelly, Mr Jim Fitzpatrick, chairman of the *Irish News*, Mr Kieran Murphy, Financial Controller, *Irish News* and Mrs Geraldine Harvey. Special thanks are due to Mr Frank Bunting, Northern Secretary of the Irish National Teachers' Organisation and to the I.N.T.O. itself for its generous donation towards the cost of publication.

Dr Eamon Phoenix edited the manuscript for publication while Mrs Kathleen Bell, Librarian, *Irish News*, Ms Linda Greenwood, Irish Studies Librarian, Belfast Central Library and Mr Roger Dixon, Librarian at the Ulster Folk and Transport Museum assisted in the quest for illustrations.

FOREWORD

BRENDAN COLGAN
Scholar and Educationalist
1933–1999

BRENDAN COLGAN WAS A SCHOLAR AND A GENTLEMAN, and I regard it as a privilege to have been asked to write a Foreword for his book on Vere Foster, so ably completed after the author's untimely death, by Dr Eamon Phoenix.

Brendan had a lifelong respect for learning, and his entire career was an education to the rest of us in making the most of the talents we have been given. As a student and primary school teacher he made a mark in the education life and times of Belfast, and as a part-time researcher and author he contributed greatly to the store of local knowledge, not least in his study of the life of Frederick Richard, the Earl of Belfast, and now in this book on Vere Foster.

He had an abiding interest in children's street games, and during his career as an assistant teacher, and then Principal of St Mary's Primary School in the Divis area of Belfast, he was able to observe at first hand how these helped to channel youthful energies into constructive activities and to develop team-work and inter-dependence. Not surprisingly this led to an award-winning television film 'Dusty Bluebells', which was later published in book form by The Blackstaff Press under the title *Let's Play*.

Brendan Colgan's educational career was the classic story of the gifted boy from the country who did well in the big city. Born in 1933 at Lisnacree, near Kilkeel, County Down, he became a boarder at St Malachy's College, Belfast at the age of 12. Sadly, however, he developed rheumatic fever during his teens, and this adversely affected his health for the rest of his life.

Taking up a business career he began work as a clerical officer in the flour mills in Corporation Street. He decided, however, that teaching was his true vocation and, with typical courage and determination, he took the then unusual step of applying for teacher-training at St Joseph's College (Trench House). After qualifying, he took a Diploma in Education at Queen's University, Belfast. Later, he won a Fellowship to the University of Ulster where, with the help of others, he developed new techniques and teaching aids through the use of video. He also served as an education adviser to the former Independent Broadcasting Authority.

Brendan's teaching career was cut short by his illness at the early age of 47. Undaunted, he continued to make a significant contribution to education and to knowledge in general, through his writings and his beautifully-crafted contributions to BBC Radio Ulster. Brendan was not only a writer and broadcaster, but also a talented artist who was, at one time, a pupil of Neil Shawcross.

He was a deeply religious man, a practising ecumenist and a devoted member of the Lamb of God Community on the Cliftonville Road in Belfast. Brendan also took part with cross-community neighbours in North Belfast in a series of monthly meetings, the memories of which are still treasured by those who noted his contribution to each gathering. Sometimes this was by way of a profound observation, or through a kind word, but Brendan always made his presence felt in a quiet, yet impressive way.

Though he made a significant contribution in his professional life to education, broadcasting and local history, Brendan Colgan also provided an outstanding example of courage, resilience and kindness in the face of an ever-present illness which taxed his physical resources severely. He cherished, and was cherished by, his devoted wife Colette and his children Patrick, Brendan and Mary Thérèse, and the wider family.

His unfailing charm, kindness and wry sense of humour impressed everyone who met him. He was invariably interested in other people's lives and work and never complained about the considerable physical burden which he himself carried. It is entirely appropriate that this, his final act of scholarship, is being published as a tribute to a devoted educationalist, and an exceptional human being.

ALF McCREARY

*Alf McCreary is an author and journalist and former Information Director at Queen's University, Belfast.

Vere Foster while in the British Diplomatic Service

PROLOGUE

O N MONDAY, CHRISTMAS EVE, 24 DECEMBER 1900, the funeral procession passing along Great Victoria Street, Belfast, in the darkening afternoon made a sombre sight. People seeing the small number of mourners behind the horse-drawn hearse would have been forgiven for thinking that it was not the funeral of anyone of importance. The short service at a simple grave in Belfast City Cemetery suggested the same.

What a false impression both conveyed. Later, the inscription on a great granite obelisk, erected at the grave, identified the deceased for passers-by. The words simply read:

In Memory
of
VERE FOSTER

BORN APRIL 26TH 1819
DIED DECEMBER 21ST 1900

Only 'Vere Foster'; not a hint that he was Vere Louis Henry Foster whose untiring work over many years had touched the lives of hundreds of thousands in the world, and especially Ireland during the darkest days of her history.

There are many who received their elementary schooling long decades after his death who will be familiar with this unique man. I was one such, long before I undertook a serious study of his life. To me, he was synonymous with my first attempts at writing and copying letters and pictures on Copy Books he had prepared. But this was only one facet of a many-faceted life.

The first Foster to settle in Ireland was a Cromwellian officer, a general, who settled on a grant of land at Dunleer in County Louth. His wife was English. Only one son, Anthony, is recorded. There are two accounts of Anthony's marriage and it seems likely that he was married twice. His first wife was Mary Verdon, a daughter of Christopher Verdon, Lord of the Manor of Clonmore in County Louth. His second marriage was to a Miss Dillon of the same county and a relative of the Bellews of Barmeath. The son of one of the marriages, John Foster was born in 1665 and married in 1704. His wife was Elizabeth, daughter of William Fortescue of Newrath, and Mary, daughter of Nicholas Gernon of Milltown, both in County Louth.

From this marriage all the subsequent members of the Foster family were descended. The first son of John and Elizabeth was Anthony, born in 1705. He was later to become the Right Hon. Anthony Foster, MP, Chief Baron of the Exchequer of Ireland.

On his death in 1778 he was succeeded by his son John Foster, MP. John became last Speaker of the Irish House of Commons from 1785 to the Act of Union in 1800. During his lifetime he parted with property in Ireland to his second son Augustus John, a diplomat, born in 1780. This was Glyde Court at Tallanstown, Ardee, County Louth. He was created a baronet of this estate in 1831. Augustus John Foster had three sons, Frederick Richard, Cavendish Hervey and Vere Louis Henry.

Thus, Vere Foster was a scion of an influential Anglo-Irish landed family. But, as we shall see in the following pages, it was his voluntary renunciation of all the privileges of his class in favour of the poor and uneducated masses of Ireland that make this man such a remarkable figure in his, and any other, epoch. His 'assisted emigration schemes', his philanthrophic efforts on behalf of education, agriculture, temperance or the upkeep of hospitals are each an heroic volume in the life of a latter-day 'Francis of Assisi' whose good deeds and example deserve never to be forgotten.

SHORTENED
GENEALOGICAL TREE
OF THE
FOSTER FAMILY

JOHN FOSTER
d 1747

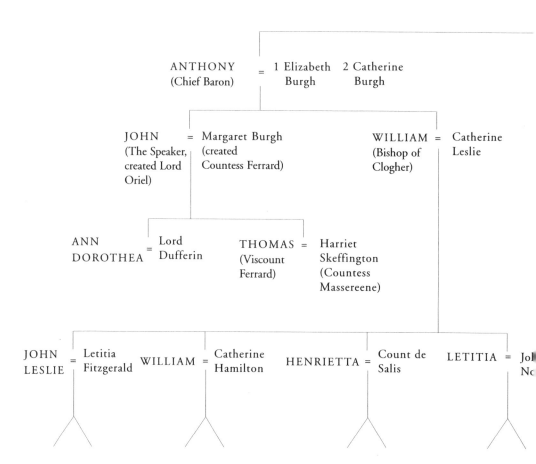

ANTHONY = 1 Elizabeth 2 Catherine
(Chief Baron)   Burgh   Burgh

JOHN = Margaret Burgh   WILLIAM = Catherine
(The Speaker, (created   (Bishop of   Leslie
created Lord   Countess Ferrard)   Clogher)
Oriel)

ANN   = Lord   THOMAS = Harriet
DOROTHEA   Dufferin   (Viscount   Skeffington
                          Ferrard)   (Countess
                                      Massereene)

JOHN = Letitia   WILLIAM = Catherine   HENRIETTA = Count de   LETITIA = Jol
LESLIE   Fitzgerald   Hamilton   Salis   No

Elizabeth Fortescue

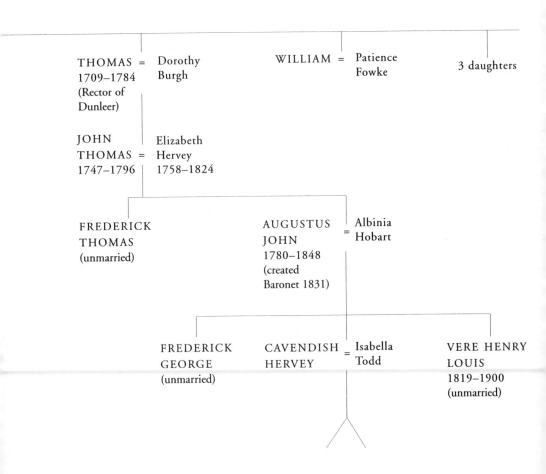

THOMAS = Dorothy
1709–1784   Burgh
(Rector of
Dunleer)

WILLIAM = Patience
                        Fowke

3 daughters

JOHN
THOMAS = Elizabeth
1747–1796   Hervey
                     1758–1824

FREDERICK
THOMAS
(unmarried)

AUGUSTUS
JOHN   = Albinia
1780–1848   Hobart
(created
Baronet 1831)

FREDERICK
GEORGE
(unmarried)

CAVENDISH = Isabella
HERVEY   Todd

VERE HENRY
LOUIS
1819–1900
(unmarried)

Branskea Castle, Dorset, opulent residence of the Foster family in the 1840s

ONE

VERE'S PRIVILEGED
EARLY LIFE

VERE LOUIS HENRY FOSTER was born in Copenhagen, Denmark, on 26 April 1819. His father, Sir Augustus Foster, had been appointed British Minister Plenipotentiary there in May 1814. In his earlier diplomatic career, Augustus had served as Secretary to the Legation of the Rt. Hon. Hugh Elliot at Naples, Minister Plenipotentiary to the United States of America and British

Minister to Sweden. His wife was Albinia Jane Hobart, daughter of the Hon. George Vere Hobart, Earl of Buckinghamshire. Their marriage took place in March 1815.

Vere Louis Henry was the youngest of their three children, all boys. Cavendish Hervey was two years older, Frederick Richard, four.

The opulence and wealth in which the boys grew up reflected the impressive list of their parents' relations and connections. Among them were the Farnans, the colourful fourth Earl of Bristol and Anglican Bishop of Derry, Viscount Palmerston, the Dufferins, Viscount Massareene and Ferrard, the Marquis of Ripon and the Duke of Devonshire. He was also a cousin of the famous Hobart Pasha, formerly Commander of the Turkish Navy.

Sir Augustus Foster, a man of importance in the British diplomatic world, never allowed work to interfere with his home life. He always brought his family with him on his postings abroad, and this resulted in it being close-knit, notwithstanding the stresses and strains of being away from home for prolonged periods. Vere was just five years old when he experienced his first family upheaval. His father was transferred from Denmark to become British Minister to Sardinia, then a small Italian kingdom. A short time later the Foster family moved into the British Embassy in Turin which soon became known simply as 'The Villa Foster'.

After his move to Turin, the education of his sons became a source of concern, indeed worry, for Augustus Foster. He wished them to have the best education possible as this would play a vital role in his plans for their futures. Consequently he arranged for all three to have private tuition, before sending them to England to board at Eton; this would entail a long boat journey twice a year. Vere was just eleven years old when he joined his brothers, 'Freddy' and 'Cavy' there. He was especially happy to have 'Freddy' again as his constant companion for they had always been good playmates, friends and confidants.

Yet, after only a short time, Vere showed signs of restlessness at Eton. His father felt he had no option but to allow him to return to Turin for private studies. This proved a wise decision and Vere, then a happy and wealthy young man, returned to England to finish his studies at his former college.

In 1838, contemplating a career in the law, Vere went up to Christ Church, Oxford. At this time he was showing no interest in joining the Diplomatic Service. Although this would have been his father's first choice for him, Sir Augustus was not unhappy at his preference for a legal career – indeed he encouraged him.

The close of the following year was a time of quiet joy for Foster's parents. Sir Augustus was about to retire as a British Ambassador and he and his wife looked forward to moving to London early in 1840. Their sons' choices of careers were also a matter for satisfaction. Frederick had joined the Diplomatic Service in 1837. His first position was a short spell under the patronage of the British Foreign Secretary, Lord Palmerston, in his office. Later he was dispatched to the embassy at Turin. His father was still in residence there and ensured that Frederick, who was appointed his secretary, received every possible help and advice. Cavendish, their second son, had determined to become a minister in the Church of England and enjoyed his parents' wholehearted support. But the Fosters were especially pleased with the progress of their youngest son. Vere appeared happy at Oxford where he continued to pursue his legal studies.

But a shock was awaiting them. Without as much as a hint to any member of the family, Vere left Oxford after less than two years. Almost immediately, he obtained work in the civil service, becoming a clerk in the Audit Offices. This was a disappointment for Sir Augustus but did nothing to dampen the warm feelings he always had for his son. There continued to be a welcome for him at the temporary London home to which the Foster parents had moved. Being an extremely popular and outgoing young man, Vere Foster had many friends. They, too, were welcome guests at the family home.

A few months after Vere's parents moved to London, word reached them that Sir Charles Chad was selling his Branskea (Brownsea) Castle and island in Poole Harbour, Dorset. They were immediately interested, aware that a former owner had transformed the castle and island into an idyllic setting. It was indeed 'a country estate extraordinary'.[1] This was the same island which the young Prince of Wales, later to become King George IV, visited in 1818. Having stepped ashore to a salutary greeting from the castle guns, he is said to have remarked, 'I had no idea that there was such a delightful spot in the kingdom'.[2]

The Fosters must have found it difficult to visualise Branskea Castle, situated on a 496 acre island, as their home. Its well-appointed apartments included a dining room 37 feet long, a saloon 24 feet long and a magnificent cruciform room commanding views from the four fronts of the castle. In addition to elegant bedrooms and a sweeping staircase, there were two drawing rooms and a large billiard room. (It was in this room that a dreadful event would take place all too soon for the family). There were many other apartments all beautifully arranged. On the island were several acres of pheasant preserve and 'Venetia Park', a three-acre walled garden for exotic plants, pineries and a sea-water swimming pool.

The family discussed the acquisition of the Branskea estate and agreed it was an opportunity too good to pass up. Sir Augustus immediately purchased it for the then enormous sum of £14,000. Aware that his family had always been accustomed to wealth and comfort, he saw the Branskea estate as a means of ensuring that they continued to live in the style which they had come to expect. Augustus had the restive Vere particularly in mind. Frederick would remain in the world of diplomacy while Cavendish was content in his London rectory, but Vere showed no signs of finding an anchor in his life. The luxury of Branskea would always be available to him as a stabilising influence.

But in 1841, less than one year after the Fosters moved into their luxury castle, Vere Foster changed the course of his life once again. He abandoned his civil service position in favour of the Diplomatic Service. Like his brother Frederick, his first assignment was to the office of the Foreign Secretary, Lord Palmerston.

From his earliest days there Vere became aware of the many idiosyncrasies in the world of diplomacy. One of Palmerston's orders was that all personnel in his department should write in copperplate. This early introduction to the importance of good handwriting made a deep impression on the young Foster and was to influence his later career in Ireland.

By 1842, Sir Augustus could draw quiet satisfaction from the fact that two of his sons had now followed his chosen path into the diplomatic corps. Frederick was now attached to the British Embassy at Dresden while Vere had just received notification of his first appointment abroad. It was as an unpaid *attaché* with Sir Henry Ellis's Mission at Rio de Janeiro, Brazil; but it was a start.[3]

On completing two extremely busy years in Rio, Vere undertook the two-and-a-half-month sea journey back to England. Following a short visit to his parents at Branskea, he and Frederick set off on a leisurely European tour which included several countries. Vere had only returned from this holiday when he learned that his next diplomatic posting was with Sir William Ouseley at Montevideo, Uruguay. Again it would be as an unpaid *attaché*. Arrangements had been made for him to sail to South America from London in December 1845.

While in Uruguay, he experienced at first hand some of the turmoil, civil war and unrest in which Britain had become involved. During the Siege of Montevideo he met the famous Garibaldi, then in command of a Genoese contingent under British protection.

From letters which he received at Branskea Castle, Sir Augustus

Foster felt his son had become too interested in the political situation in South America. Not only did Vere express such thoughts in his letters to his father, but his forthright views on liberty and his condemnation of Rosas, the South American dictator, were being made more and more public. Sir Augustus wrote to Palmerston requesting leave of absence for Vere. At the same time, he appealed to his son not to become involved in partisanship as his position did not allow for this. Finally, his father requested him to leave the Diplomatic Service and recommence reading for the Bar. These pleadings were in vain, so it was with feelings of relief Sir Augustus learned in June 1847 that the British Embassy at Montevideo had been instructed to close. In a short time Sir William Ouseley, Vere Foster and other members of the small staff returned to London.

While the young diplomat's views and statements on the political situation in Uruguay may have caused some embarrassment to London, the Foreign Office was keenly aware of Vere's qualities as a budding diplomat and his capacity for hard work. As a result, he was promoted to the position of a paid *attaché* at the British Embassy in Buenos Aires, Argentina.

The Foreign Office was therefore taken aback when Foster declined this superior position. He did not offer his resignation then, but coming events would dictate that his career in the British Diplomatic Service would soon end permanently.

The Foster residence, Glyde Court, County Louth

TWO

FIRST EXPERIENCES
OF IRELAND'S AGONY

FOLLOWING HIS RETURN FROM MONTEVIDEO IN 1847, Vere Foster proceeded almost immediately to Branskea. There he was disappointed to find his father unwell. He learned that this illness had commenced shortly after Sir Augustus moved into the castle.

But Vere discovered him full of interest in the outside world. Their conversations often turned to Ireland and the Foster property there, near Ardee in County Louth. Although Augustus had visited his picturesque Irish estate, Glyde Court, on a number of occasions, he did not settle there. Like many other members of the Anglo-Irish landed gentry, he decided to remain an absentee landlord.

Absentee landlords lived mostly outside Ireland but some resided in other large mansions which they owned elsewhere. They usually employed land agents to see to the affairs of their estates and, in particular, to ensure the collection of rents from the tenants. If the tenants were unable to pay their rents the land agents often had their thatched houses or cabins demolished. This sadly resulted in their occupants being thrown on to the roadside without any shelter.

Not all landlords fell into this category, however, and Sir Augustus was among those who set out to ensure that none of his tenants would be treated in such a callous manner. He instructed his land agent in County Louth to keep him informed of all happenings at Glyde Court and to forward any requests from tenants for financial assistance in the upkeep of their homes or farms. These requests were seldom, if ever, refused. Tenants were also assured of freedom to practise their religion openly. Although himself a Protestant, Augustus Foster had been one of the most ardent supporters of the Catholic Emancipation Act, passed at Westminster in 1829, which allowed Catholics to sit in parliament for the first time.

The tenants of Glyde Court, being on the country's east coast, were spared the early effects of the horrific potato blight when it struck Ireland in 1845. The parts initially affected were mostly along the south-west, west and north-west coastlines. Sir Augustus had instructed his agent to send him copies of the Irish newspapers to inform him of Irish affairs. However, the contemporary papers carried conflicting reports of the blight's arrival. One misleading report ran:

> ... Happily there is no ground for any apprehension of the kind (potato failure) in Ireland. There may have been partial failures in

some localities; but we believe that there never was a more abundant potato crop in Ireland than there is at present, and none which it will be more likely to secure.

Only six weeks later, however, on 22 October 1845, a Belfast newspaper, *The Vindicator*, painted a very different picture:

> The failure of the potato crop in Ireland, which has for some time been feared, is now confirmed by circumstantial accounts from almost all parts of the country. A large portion of the crop turns out to be quite useless for purposes of food. A dearth is inevitable and a famine is extremely probable.

A failure of the potato crop in Ireland is a calamity of the greatest magnitude. The Irish peasantry rely almost exclusively on potatoes for their subsistence; and when the crop fails, they have nothing to fall back upon but grass, nettles and seaweed [1]

It was not until Vere Foster returned from South America that he learned about the potato failure in Ireland. His father and Frederick were familiar with the disaster and it caused them much distress. Vere listened to details of the blight and famine from both, especially Frederick. Although on Foreign Office duty in Europe, Frederick had paid a number of visits to Ireland earlier on his father's behalf and heard first-hand accounts of the sufferings of the affected areas.

Vere was greatly disturbed by his brother's reports. Indeed, he had no need to search further for information on the famine, poverty, emigration and the abominable conduct of many landlords in Ireland than in newspaper articles in *The Illustrated London News* and the *Times*. The *Illustrated London News* reported on 29 August 1846:

> The potato has been attacked by a new disease, the nature of which is unknown, which speedily destroys the hopes of the farmer and even converts whole fields of potatoes into a mass of corruption within a

few hours. What is very remarkable is that the most healthy and vigorous potato-fields are those which are destroyed most rapidly. Not a sign of the disease may be seen today, tomorrow the leaves may be withered, black and half-putrid.[2]

By April 1847 the stream of emigrants from Ireland to British cities was graphically reported in the *Times*:

> Among the crimes charged against Irish Landlords none has aroused more resentment in Britain early in 1847 than what is seen as the dumping ground of their evicted pauper tenants on the shores of England, Scotland and Wales ... a swelling tide of Irish immigrants in Britain most of them very poor and many of them diseased. Liverpool took the brunt of this so-called invasion with as many as 50,000 pouring into (that port) during the month of March '47 alone. Many of these new arrivals died on the streets or crowded into hospitals or workhouses.[3]

As the Great Famine reached catastrophic proportions in 'Black '47', the *Times* was unsparing in its condemnation of British government policy and the landed class:

> ... Through its persistent neglect (since the Act of Union), wealthy Britain had permitted in Ireland a mass of poverty, disaffection and degradation without parallel in the world. It allowed proprietors to suck the very life blood of that wretched race.[4]

It was against the background of this unfolding tragedy that Vere Foster became directly involved with Ireland. His life was changed forever.

He was at Branskea when his father received a plea from the land agent at Glyde Court on behalf of one of his tenants. The man needed financial assistance to help him emigrate to America. Sir Augustus, having no previous experience of anything relating to emigration, asked

Vere to cross over to Ardee and arrange it. Vere willingly agreed to go. Not only would this be Vere's first visit to Ireland but also a first-hand introduction to its suffering and the scandalous tragedies related to emigration. He was just twenty-eight years old.

The staff at Glyde Court were informed of his expected date of arrival so a coach and pair awaited him as he disembarked from a sailing ship at Drogheda port. Vere became aware at once of the vast throng of people waiting at the quayside to embark on vessels like the one on which he had sailed from England. The majority of them appeared desperately emaciated and forlorn. These he recognised as impoverished emigrants escaping starvation and disease.

The young Englishman witnessed similar scenes on the short coach journey from the port to Glyde Court. People, singly and in groups, were making their melancholy way, some with donkey or horse and cart, but mostly on foot, to the quayside. They had with them what appeared to be all their earthly belongings.

Foster's first experiences of Ireland were thus heart-rending. Although he saw no signs of crop failure in County Louth there were many people appallingly ill, travelling along its narrow roads. He drew some consolation, however, from the knowledge that money, rice and grain had been donated by members of the Foster family, ensuring that no one on or near the Glyde Court estate died from want or starvation.

Young Foster's mind was still far from ease as his coach arrived at the simple gatehouse of Glyde Court. The coach swung into the winding driveway and, while making its way to the fine Georgian house, passed under a canopy of high trees. Glyde Court immediately appealed to him. As he surveyed its long elevation and Tudor-style architecture, Vere would have been aware that the English writer, Thackeray had extolled the mansion in his *Irish Sketchbook* of 1843. A later architectural historian noted:

The entrance was on the North front which had two gable-ends flanking an arcade of three pointed arches against a two storey front with a sham gable above. The West front had a thirteen-bay façade with two large three-bay bows and numerous sham gables and many stacks.[5]

Vere soon became familiar with its great interior beauty: the splendid dining room and delightfully furnished drawing room. Most of the apartments looked out on to manicured lawns adorned with flowers, roses, shrubs and trees. The wide spiral staircase led up to a majestic master bedroom. The servants' quarters were at the rear. Outside, besides the vegetable garden and orchards, stood the courtyard with stabling for the riding and chaise horses. Other houses stored coaches, hansoms, traps, harness and the like. The grooms' quarters were nearby.

Vere thought that he might like to reside at Glyde Court eventually. But he had not come to stay but to arrange the emigration details of a tenant on the estate, so Foster set about this task. In doing so, he had his first personal experience of the dreadful emigration traffic between Drogheda and Liverpool.

At an Emigration Agent's Office (there were other similar offices at ports along the Irish coastlines), he paid the tenant's full fare of £4. 10s. (£4.50p) to America. This entitled holders to travel across the Irish Sea to Liverpool. There they would transfer to an American-bound vessel. Additional large vessels were moored and ready to sail to other ports and countries for those who had chosen to emigrate there.

Vere learned that many would-be emigrants were unable to pay their full fares to the New World. They even had difficulty in finding the half-crown (12$\frac{1}{2}$p) for a ticket to Liverpool. The fare for members of the upper class – like Foster himself – from Drogheda to Liverpool, was 10 shillings (50p). This secured travel in a private cabin with the attention of a steward. Foster had soon need of his ticket as urgent word reached him at Glyde Court that his father had become seriously ill.

Thoughts of the widespread horrors in many parts of Ireland crowded Vere's mind as he set sail for Branskea. He may have been leaving these suffering people but his heart remained among them. With a strong desire to return and render what help he could, he boarded a typical sailing ship bound for Liverpool, on to which emigrants were crowding. Although shown to his cabin Vere did not remain there but chose to cross the Irish Sea in the emigrants' section of the ship. He was appalled at their deprivation and had no doubt that the teeming numbers on deck, plus those below, were blatantly far in excess of what the ship was capable of holding. This human cargo comprised young and old, male and female. In addition, and sharing the same accommodation, were animals, cattle and horses in pens and make-shift sheds. To his horror, given the hunger in Ireland at this time, the vessel also contained barrels of wheat and firkins of butter.

Sea-sickness was prevalent among the passengers during the entire journey. The resultant odours (for there were no toilet or washing facilities) mingled with those of animal and human excrement. It was a blessed relief when, at the end of a slow journey across the Irish Sea, the ship finally cast anchor at Liverpool.

NOW IN PORT.
NOTICE TO PASSENGERS.

Those Persons who have taken their Passages by the First Class Coppered Ship

SUPERIOR,
CAPTAIN MASON,
FOR QUEBEC,

Are required to be in Derry on TUESDAY, the 13th of JULY, pay the remainder of their Passage Money, and go on Board, as the Vessel will sail first fair wind after that date. A few more Passengers will be taken, on moderate terms, if immediate application is made to

Mr. DAVID MITCHELL, *Dungiven,* or the Owners.

J. & J. COOKE.

Derry, June 28, 1847.

☞ The Cargo of the SUPERIOR, just arrived, from *Philadelphia,* consisting of Indian Corn, Indian Meal, Flour, &c., for Sale, on moderate terms.

BUCHANAN, PRINTER.

Shipping companies often used misleading advertisement
to lure unwary emigrants

Runners waiting at the quayside

THREE

CRIMPS, RUNNERS,
MAN-CATCHERS AND PORTERS

SHOULD THE EMIGRANTS HAVE FELT as they prepared to disembark with their belongings that the groups and individuals gathered at the quayside were there to welcome and help them, they were horribly mistaken. Vere was quickly to learn that the 'welcoming parties' were instead the best organised sets of confidence tricksters imaginable. This bunch of rogues comprised 'porters', 'runners', 'crimps' and 'man-catchers'. All were intent on separating the emigrants from what little savings or possessions they carried. Because they worked on handsome commissions for shipping agents, brokers, shop-keepers and owners of lodging-houses, these extortionists were not only wealthy but violent. Vere observed them carefully then and immediately began studying their *modus operandi*.

Working to well-prepared plans, porters and runners set their sights on the bewildered and frightened emigrants as they arrived. Porters suddenly appeared and dragged the emigrants' baggage off the ship. They then demanded money, which the owners usually gave them, for its release. Runners, on the other hand, cunningly snatched any luggage left unattended on the quayside and made off with it. To try and retrieve their worldly possessions the owners were forced to dash after the thieves. Sometimes hand-to-hand fighting resulted when they caught up with them. Some emigrants were forced to follow the run-ners, still holding on to their luggage, to filthy lodging-houses where the runners received a handsome rake-off from the proprietors. There they were forced to stay in fear and in atrocious conditions. To make the emigrants remain in these fever-ridden dens their belongings were often confiscated or even sold. There were no means of escape from these foul, overcrowded lodging-houses, many owned by shipping com-panies which often made extra money by altering the shipping arrange-ments of the emigrants they had captured, to later dates.

As the *Liverpool Albion* noted on 15 May 1850:

> 'Men, women and children would be bedded down together, often on
> a cold stone floor, without any blankets. Here the emigrants would be
> often robbed, cheated, over-charged and run the very considerable
> risk of contracting a variety of contagious diseases.'[1]

Cholera was one such disease. Its cause was contact with human excre-ment and the use of chamber pots which had not been washed or emptied for long periods. They slept in unclean, unchanged beds which other passengers had used on previous nights and continued picking up various diseases and spreading them. Forty-six children under four years old died of measles on one voyage of the *Marco Polo* because of one child who had come on board after sleeping in a Liverpool lodging-house.[2]

Crimps carried out their wily tasks in many ways. One was by selling tickets for an onward journey to unsuspecting emigrants who had only bought tickets to Liverpool. For this crimps also received a hefty commission from passenger-brokers and lodging-house owners. They continually persuaded emigrants to have their money changed for that of the country to which they were going. The foreign coin received was usually almost worthless. Vere witnessed one migrant part with ten pounds – it appeared to be his total savings – for ten United States cents which the crimp assured his victim was of the same value.

At the quayside crimps purported to sell large tracts of land in the United States or Canada to unsuspecting emigrants. Needless to say, these rogues did not own that land so the alleged title deed was of no value. Yet many were swindled of much of the little money they had, to buy it.

Vere learned about other abominable actions carried out against unsuspecting emigrants at Liverpool. Should they have been fortunate enough to escape the attentions of the crimps, they were likely to fall into the clutches of the man-catchers. These swindlers cunningly duped emigrants into believing they could provide them with cheap sailing tickets at the offices of certain passenger-brokers. Usually successful, the man-catchers brought their victims to equally unscrupulous brokers who charged exorbitant sums. The tricksters were paid a hefty commission for each 'catch'.

Many poor emigrants suffered at the hands of unscrupulous lodging-house owners who arranged for them to steal aboard trans-Atlantic ships as stowaways. They were concealed in chests, boxes or barrels with air holes which they were assured would prevent suffocation. Victims of this trickery were promised that, once out to sea, they might escape from their containers and continue their journeys unnoticed. They were never informed that this was impossible because of continuous searchings by ships' crews for stowaways. Numerous unfortunates were found dead from suffocation, their make-shift containers serving as their coffins.

Local straw depots and grocers' shops cajoled innocent emigrants into buying bales of straw which they lied to them would be necessary and sufficient for a month's bedding during their sea journey. Similarly, hardware shops sold them pots, utensils and goods at inflated prices they could ill afford. Many were lucky to get on board with even a few pounds or shillings left.

Emigrants often suffered because they could not understand the English language; Irish was the only language spoken by a large number passing through Liverpool and other English ports. Failure to speak or understand English was obviously a real obstacle in these completely strange surroundings.

Vere remained in Liverpool longer than he had planned as travelling directly to his ill father at Branskea had been his original intention. He witnessed emigrants turning in despair to the city's Protestant and Catholic churches for help. Although much aid was given, the churches found it almost impossible to satisfy the never-ending demands made on them.

The streets of Liverpool, especially those near the docks, were scenes of human misery at its most poignant. Vere witnessed people lying huddled together for warmth in doorways of houses in the airless streets, courts and cellars. One of the most slum-infested districts which Foster came upon was Curry Street, where emigrants faced squalor, the lack of any sanitation and a scarcity of drinking water.

Vere later learned that in one year (1850), 568 ships, all packed to the gunwales with emigrants, sailed out of Liverpool. On one morning tide 16 ships weighed anchor, leaving behind them swarming, pulsating crowds of disappointed men, women and frightened children who had been too many for the last of those 16 ships. They went back into the dirty streets along the waterfront, hoping to sail on the next daylight tide, once again crowding into the verminous lodging-houses.

Many bewildered migrants had no opportunities to enquire about the ships on which they would travel to North America, Australia or the like. Most information was gleaned from the walls of buildings placarded with notices and names of shipping companies. These included *INMAN ROYAL MAIL STEAMERS, HARDEN & CO., TAPSCOTT BROS.*, and *WHITE STAR LINE*, relating to their packet ships, destinations and dates of sailings. Vere, with his experience of transatlantic journeys, was aware that much of the information thus disseminated was patently false. One advertisement related to a vessel, the *Sea Nymph*, soon to sail from Liverpool to Canada and illustrates the flagrant use of fantasy and illusion to entice the unsuspecting to use that ship:

> After being fifteen or twenty days out, the ship will probably be within the influence of the gulf-stream. A little cooling medicine, or a jug of salt water, may not be amiss. The ship is by this time 'half-seas over'. If you are going to Quebec, you will now be approaching the banks of Newfoundland and will perhaps be catching your own codfish and observing occasionally the spouting of a whale; the rising and setting sun, the brilliancy of the night, falling stars; the sporting schools of bonitos; the occasional falling on board of flying-fish; landbirds settling on the rigging, so fatigued as to be caught by the sailors; dolphins racing as it were with the vessel …[3]

Vere found this type of seductive and inaccurate propaganda, along with false descriptions of vessels and their capacity, reprehensible. His resentment was most intense when he witnessed swarming crowds waiting to embark at the docks. There were also many who appeared disappointed and angry, having been swindled out of sailing on the ships for which they had paid their fares to passenger-brokers. Once, Vere made his way to the Government Emigrant Agent to complain about these abuses. He found the official helpful, acknowledging that it was his duty to see to the welfare of all emigrants passing through the port. As regards the 21 passenger-brokers and ship-owners then operating in Liverpool, the agent was aware that many were dishonest but pleaded that it was almost impossible to apprehend them.

Vere Foster's mind was in turmoil as he left Liverpool after his one-week sojourn and travelled on to Branskea. While on Foreign Office duties he had experienced difficulties, problems and unrest in countries abroad; now he had become acquainted with some of the agonies being suffered by countless thousands on his own doorstep. He was appalled at what he had learned and resolved to make emigrants aware of the steps which they must take to protect themselves as they set out. One idea he considered feasible was the preparation of a set of 'help and advice notices'. This he incorporated in his *Work and Wages* pamphlets published later. In part of a section entitled 'How to engage your passage', he warned the Irish emigrant:

> At Liverpool, or any other port of embarkation for America, be careful whom you employ to show you a shipping office; ask no questions in the street, pay no attention to the offers of service of anyone you meet, not even to ask your way to any place or office ...[4]

However, sad events within the Foster family prevented Vere proceeding with these plans as urgently he would have wished.

FOUR

A FAMILY TRAGEDY
AND THE CALL OF IRELAND

O N HIS ARRIVAL AT BRANSKEA CASTLE Vere found his father in seriously declining health. Frederick was with him, having hurriedly returned – at their mother's request – from diplomatic duties in Venice. Sir Augustus had begun falling into bouts of depression and Vere joined Frederick in an attempt to lift his spirits.

When opportunity allowed, the two Foster sons shared their knowledge of the Glyde Court estate in County Louth with its farms and

21

tenants as they had found them. They discovered a mutual interest: each had a deep desire to alleviate the needs of the tenantry, indeed of people everywhere in Ireland. They even discussed some remedial actions they might undertake. But their plans had to be placed in abeyance as Frederick received a call to return to Venice as soon as possible.

Vere decided to remain at Branskea, so Frederick left with an easy mind. He was confident of Vere's ability to deal with any problems on their Irish estate. Since nothing untoward did happen, Vere was able to remain close to his ailing father. At the same time, he acquainted himself with all information available regarding the overall situation in Ireland.

Vere's Foreign Office experience was not wasted and he was able to learn from British Parliamentary Papers and other reports that during a single month, April 1847, 56,000 emigrants, almost all from Ireland, had sailed into British ports. Liverpool, which he had experienced so recently at first hand, handled 24,000. Of this number, 14,471 sailed to the United States, the remainder to British colonies.

Further incredible information which he obtained relating to these early years of *An Gorta Mor* ('The Great Hunger'), concerned shipments of food from Ireland to England. During the week commencing 30 October 1846, exactly one year before his first visit to Glyde Court, exports into the port of Liverpool from Ireland included 1,952 sacks of flour, 190 sacks of oats, 50 barrels of barley, 2,256 barrels of oats, 1,078 baskets of butter, 21 tons of oatmeal, 332 bales of bacon and 10,179 firkins of butter. During the same week similar shipments were made from Ireland to the port of Bristol and, in November 1846, exports to London included 4,597 tierces and hampers of bacon, 29,526 packages of butter and 1,496 packages of pork. These did not include animals for slaughter which were carried on board almost every ship packed with emigrants.

Vere found it impossible to understand why these huge quantities of foodstuff were allowed to leave from Ireland while several millions of its people were either starving or subsisting on morsels of food, of the poorest quality.

At this time Vere learned, and the Glyde Court agent confirmed, that parts of County Louth had been affected by fever and dysentery of an alarming and malignant character. The area around the Foster estate had not yet suffered but Vere and the agent were fearful of what might happen to the tenantry should that scourge come among them.

Vere learned much of the plight of the Irish people through descriptive notes and sketches by James Mahony of Cork in *The Illustrated London News*. Mahony was an artist commissioned by that newspaper to confirm the accuracy of accounts in Irish provincial papers of the extent of the suffering and starvation in those areas worst affected by the famine. A typical report from Mahony read:

> ... We first proceeded to Bridgetown (Co Cork) ... and there I saw the dying, the living and the dead, lying indiscriminately upon the same floor, without anything between them and the cold earth, save a few miserable rags upon them. To point to any particular house as a proof of this would be a waste of time, as all were in the same state ...[1]

The information which Foster obtained on the catastrophe developing in Ireland while at Branskea affected him greatly, distressed though he was at his father's illness. Indeed, he was filled with feelings of pessimism for Ireland's future.

Meanwhile, Sir Augustus Foster was suffering recurring bouts of depression and constantly confided to Vere his fears for the survival of religion in a rapidly changing world. Often these thoughts took precedence over all others and it appeared as if they were becoming unbearable for him. Sir Augustus's fits of depression became more frequent and more intense.

Despite assiduous medical care and his son's devoted attention, Augustus Foster's health continued to decline. But no one at Branskea could have anticipated the circumstances of his death on 1 August 1848. In what must have been a period of extreme mental agony, Sir Augustus committed suicide by slitting his throat. He was found in the billiard room. *The Gentleman Magazine* of September 1848 recorded the tragedy:

> Sir Augustus Foster Bt; at an inquest held on the body of the deceased, it appears that he had been suffering from a disease of the heart and lungs and had recently laboured under a delirium, during a fit of which he destroyed himself by cutting his throat. A verdict was returned of temporary insanity.

The family were shattered, but they had the love and support of each other to carry them through this period of shock and distress. The burial of Sir Augustus took place in Studland Churchyard, south of Poole Harbour and arrangements were made for a monument to be erected over his grave. All expenses of their father's funeral were recorded by Vere in a 'red marbled notebook'.[2]

Following the obsequies, Lady Albinia remained at Branskea Castle while Rev Cavendish and his wife returned to their parish residence in London. Frederick and Vere, while promising every support to their mother in the future, had no plans to reside in the majestic castle. In a short time, Frederick, having inherited his father's baronetcy, severed his connections with the Diplomatic Service and crossed to Glyde Court. His Irish tenants were pleased at his coming, knowing that he possessed much of his late father's kindness towards them.

Vere, still officially on the staff of the Foreign Office, was posted to the British Embassy in Brussels where Lord Walden was Minister. But he had no wish to stay in that post. Ireland was constantly on his mind, a land ravaged by three years of famine, fever, emigration and death. Having personally experienced some of its sufferings, he felt more and more drawn to the country, increasingly convinced that his future must be spent there. He was also certain that this was what his father would have wished him to do, not least in view of his humane treatment and solicitude towards his tenants during his lifetime.

In a lecture in Rosemary Street Lecture Hall, Belfast, on 28 January 1879, Vere Foster described how he took this momentous decision:

> The last diplomatic mission, with which I was connected in South America, having been suspended and the Irish Famine occurring at the same time, I determined to take up my residence in Ireland in the hope of making myself useful by falling in with any practical scheme for giving increased employment to the people and participating against a recurrence of similar sufferings in the future ...

As a result, he concluded a final one month appointment in Brussels with the Diplomatic Service before returning to his mother at Branskea. Frederick, then settled at Glyde Court, was not surprised to receive an early request from his brother to join him there. He assured Vere of a warm welcome to their Irish estate.

Upon Vere's arrival, the two brothers began investigating extensively the living conditions and sufferings of the Irish people in all its forms. They also considered how and where they might give assistance to local relief schemes. Realising that the Famine was most searing in the south and west of the country, they decided to work in these parts after they had acquainted themselves of the precise circumstances and most efficacious way of assisting the population. They agreed, however, that a postponement of a tour there, would be necessary until after Queen Victoria's visit to Ireland, scheduled for August of that year, 1849. Sir Frederick, because of his regard for the Queen, his position in Irish society and his role as High Sheriff at the Assizes in Dundalk, had planned to journey to Dublin for the royal festivities. Vere, while himself an admirer of Victoria, would not join Frederick in Dublin. His plan was to spend the duration of the royal visit with his mother at Branskea Castle.

Victoria had already acknowledged the existence of a crisis in Ireland. An English newspaper, the *Daily News* of 10 January 1847 noted that the Queen 'aware of the famines in Ireland and Scotland, donated £2,000 and Prince Albert £500, to the Irish and Scottish Relief Society.' A decision, however, was made in 1849 that ' ... a Royal visit should be organised to rally morale and show Royal sympathy to Queen Victoria's Irish subjects.[3]

The *Illustrated London News*, while praising Her Majesty's proposed visit to Ireland as an event of national importance, queried certain aspects of it:

> The Queen will not see the dark side of Ireland. She will not behold with her own eyes the wretchedness of the peasantry, the fertile acres lying uncultivated for want of capital and of skill – the roofless cabins of myriads of homeless people and the vast tracts of land that have never been turned by plough or spade, nor yielded food for human kind. She will see, it has been said, the bright side only. She will hear the thunder of artillery and shouting of the multitude and not the wail of distress and sickness that comes from the roadside or from the interior of the miserable cabins ... But though, in all probability she will neither hear nor see, she is not ignorant of these things when she goes to Ireland.[4]

The royal visit was a success but at no time did the party witness any of Ireland's wretchedness or suffering because of the nature of the official itinerary. The experiences were as satisfactory and equal in every way as in any other part of the Union. They travelled through the Phoenix

Park from the Viceregal Lodge in an open barouche and along the River Liffey by the Strawberry Beds. They enjoyed the sylvan beauty of Woodlands, the splendid seat of Colonel White at which a triumphal arch of flowering shrubs had been erected in honour of her Majesty; they visited the town of Leixlip, Co Kildare, near which Victoria and her entourage were cheered by the student priests of Maynooth College; they made a visit to Carton demesne and mansion where the royal party were entertained to one of the most sumptuous meals of the tour; the distinguished guests partook inside while the accompanying visitors, including Sir Frederick Foster, were entertained in the special marquees on the lawns. Following the banquet, a display of Irish jigs, to the accompaniment of the music of an Irish piper, was arranged for the sovereign on the front lawn.

Happiness and contentment permeated the entire Irish visit and at its conclusion, the royals, their party and other members of the nobility, returned to their domains. Sir Frederick, back in the opulence of Glyde Court, was soon joined by Vere from Branskea.

But they were soon to exchange – for a short time – their world of wealth and ease for one of unimaginable poverty and distress.

A starving mother and her famished children:
Vere Foster encountered many such scenes on his
tour of Ireland in 1847.

FIVE

THE FOSTERS' TOUR
OF IRELAND'S SOUTH AND WEST

THE KNOWLEDGE WHICH THE FOSTER BROTHERS already
had about the afflictions and sufferings of the inhabitants of
the southern and western counties of Ireland was confirmed at
the commencement of their journey.

Everywhere they were horrified by the sight of people with sunken
faces and perishing bodies wasted by hunger, disease and privation. At

least half of them seemed to have only one-room mud cabins of the worst description in which to live. Built by the owners themselves, the walls were of clay, stone and thatch. Many hovels were roofless. Windows and doors were nothing more than holes in the walls and were often covered over by boards to keep out wind and rain when necessary. Open turf fires provided heat not only for the cold, draughty hovels but also for cooking in the large iron cooking-pots. Sadly many families did not possess this basic utensil as it cost more than they could afford.

> They were paying five pence a stone for diseased potatoes when they could scrape together enough to buy some; but, as they had no work, this was a rare occurrence, and the whole family might be said to be living on casual charity. An earl, to relieve distress, had purchased half a ton of Indian meal, which was retailed at two pence per pound to his starving tenantry. This nobleman contrives to squeeze from the 'roofless cabins' and elsewhere nearly £40,000 a year.[1]

Where furniture existed it was crude and home-made. Beds were usually bundles of straw, and if none was available, the family slept on the mud floors. A sheep very often shared the family accommodation.

Stench was everywhere because of the complete lack of drainage and sanitation and the piles of manure close to almost all the hovels. Disease in every form was, therefore, widespread, often resulting in whole families being wiped out.

An incredible sight for the Fosters was the number of cabins pulled down while their dead occupants still lay inside. Some had died of fever and no one, even close relations or friends, dared enter in case they were infected. Peasants who had left their diseased or fever-ridden hovels, or had no homes at all, often made abodes or cavities in hillsides where gravel and stones had been dug out.

Alongside the hovels was land which was usually sub-divided into very small farms. Sometimes these were as large as fifteen acres, but the majority were only five acres or less – mere 'potato gardens'. These marginalized tenant farmers and cottiers were incapable of producing sufficient crops to sustain their families and meet the rent demands of their landlords.

Another group of people, the most dispirited and worn out of all, were the 'spalpeens'. These day-labourers, girls and men, could find work for approximately half of any year. This came usually from two sources – helping to repair roads or working on neighbouring farms.

The Fosters found that in some districts agricultural labour of one form or another was available in the landlord's demesnes. Yearly wages for men who could find this employment was £3 to £6 while, for girls, it was £1 to £3. However, the rate depended on the local landlord. One in particular, the Marquis of Hertford, was widely known to draw an annual ground rent of £60,000. He paid wages so low that there was nothing but hunger and distress on his estates; destitute tenants who could not afford to pay the exorbitant rents were evicted. The Fosters were justly horrified just as their father had been before them; towards the end of his life, in December 1847, Sir Augustus Foster had record-ed his disgust at such unchristian treatment in his diary:

> I think it might be attended with the best effects if such actions were publicly advertised to exist and then Irish landlords were to be heavi-ly fined who eject poor people and throw them on their neighbours.[2]

The peasants could not be blamed, therefore, for allowing their patch-es of land to lie waste and uncultivated. The reality was widespread hunger and never-ending endeavours to exist on detestable diets. The Fosters, already familiar with reports of this destitution, were now wit-nessing the appalling spectacle for themselves. Typical was the follow-ing description published in the Belfast *Vindicator* in December 1846 and copied from the *Cork Examiner* of the previous Friday:

Disease and death in every quarter – the once hardy population worn away to emaciated skeletons – fever, dropsy, diarrhoea and famine in every filthy hovel, and sweeping away whole families – hundreds rushing from their homes and country – dead bodies of children flung into holes hastily scratched in the earth, without shroud or coffin – wives travelling ten miles to beg the charity of a coffin for a dead husband and bearing it back that weary distance – every field becoming a grave and the land a wilderness …[3]

Several thousand emigrated, principally to England, being too poor to proceed to America or Canada and at least 6,000 perished by starvation. In Connacht there remained a miserable remnant of little more than 20,000, of whom 10,000 were on the verge of starvation living upon turnip-tops, sand-eels and seaweed, a diet which no one in England would have considered fit for the meanest of domestic animal.

In some areas there was grave distrust between landlord and tenant. The landlord suspected that, if he gave seed for sowing, the tenant would consume the crop and not pay him for his rent; the tenant, for his part, feared that if he sowed the seed, the landlord would seize the crop as soon as it was harvested. This distrust was yet another reason for little farms remaining uncultivated and the tenants emigrating.

With some relief the Fosters came upon some estates owned by landowners who paid their tenants six pence per day to drain and improve their bogland farms. As a result, their new land was producing soil very suitable for small crops of turnips, parsnips, corn or other greens.

Seeing this land improvement, Frederick and Vere discussed how they could promote similar schemes for the transformation of infertile land. They were aware of a speech given by the Presbyterian Young Irelander, John Martin to the Confederate Club in Newry, County Down, on 27 December 1847, in which he argued that if the whole question of Irish agriculture were properly managed, sufficient food could be grown for at least twenty million people each year. Although he had no knowledge of agriculture, Vere Foster was particularly interested in improving arable land. It would be necessary, therefore, to seek advice. Even before this, he had considered the possibility of purchasing a large farm in the west of Ireland and employing qualified advisers to educate local peasants in basic farming techniques.

Apart from tenant farmers with very little land there were innumerable others who were penniless, without even a garden; they too had been evicted by landlords or their agents. Dispossessed of their cabins, they were left to wander the countryside or make their way to the nearest workhouse. James H Tuke, who visited Connacht in the autumn of 'Black '47', noted:

> Between 1846 and 1849, 160,000 people were evicted from their holdings in Ireland. Some of these unfortunates, wrote Spencer Walpole in his *History of England*, crowded into the Irish workhouses and the deaths in these buildings, week for week, equalled the deaths in the whole of London with its two million inhabitants. Others of them lay down and died on the roadside ... Wherever they went, with them went the seed of disease.[4]

Fever was rampant in scores of workhouses and the fever sheds and tents built specially for the sufferers were overcrowded. Death was a regular visitor and chutes were used to drop corpses from higher storeys down to the large, open, coffinless graves below. The bodies were forever at the mercy of marauding dogs. Fever, cholera, typhus and other diseases had spread like wildfire among the afflicted due to the fact that often upwards on six to eight people were sleeping in one bed.

All the workhouses the Fosters visited were packed with people while many more sought to gain entry. This was despite these unfortunates knowing that discipline inside was deliberately severe. Typical work for men consisted of breaking stones, unravelling ropes and the fumigation of rooms for clothes and bedding. Work for women included washing, cooking and cleaning. Some inmates decided to leave or escape from workhouses because of their atrocious conditions. Sadly this resulted in families being split up.

The Fosters calculated that almost two thirds of those in the workhouses were children and young people, very many of them orphans. There were no signs of even the most basic rudiments of education being available for these unfortunate youngsters. The sombre uniforms which inmates wore contributed to the dismal atmosphere of the workhouse. One contemporary commentator noted:

> It is probable there are, at least, 30,000 children under sixteen years of age in the thirty Union workhouses of Ireland. Although it is by no means intended to be inferred that the whole are untaught, yet it is a fact that a large number are either inefficiently taught or wholly uneducated.[5]

Frederick and Vere concluded that most Irish children received little or no education while condemned to remain in workhouses. However Vere Foster's concept of education was something wider than the basics of early classroom skills; it should have a rich curriculum comprising handicrafts, trades, agricultural training and skills for appropriate age ranges. Provision of a varied education for young people would thus better equip them for life and possible future employment.

The most deplorable workhouse and local distress to be experienced by Vere and Frederick was in Swinford Union, County Mayo. Although built to hold 700 people, 820 were quickly admitted and hundreds more were refused entry for lack of accommodation. As a result some died on roads and in nearby fields. The Fosters could not detect any improvement at all on an earlier Relief Committee's figures relating to deaths in Swinford and other workhouses in County Mayo:

Swinford Workhouse: 367 deaths

Ballina Workhouse: 1150 deaths including the Medical Officer of the House

Ballinrobe Workhouse: 254 deaths and all the officers of the House.[6]

Such deaths as well as the terror of infectious diseases and the actions of many landlords and their agents in Swinford drove people to abandon that area of Mayo completely.

There was little difference at that time between Counties Mayo and Cork. On 18 December 1846, the *Cork Examiner* newspaper carried this description of the unspeakable situation in the county:

> Disease and death in every quarter – the once hardy population worn away to emaciated skeletons – fever, dropsy, diarrhoea and famine: rioting in every filthy hovel, and sweeping away whole families: hundreds rushing from their home and country: dead bodies of children flung into holes hastily scratched in the earth without shroud or coffin: wives travelling ten miles to beg the charity of a coffin for a dead husband, and bearing it back that weary distance: every field becoming a grave and the land a wilderness …

The Foster brothers had become only too familiar with such scenes during their tour of County Cork. Some farmers who owned a small acreage of land often parted with it for much less than its worth. They were then able to afford the emigration fares to North America or Australia with their families. People with almost no property and money also left their local areas hoping to find a happier existence elsewhere. The majority, who wanted to emigrate to America, were condemned to travel there in 'coffin ships' leaving from ports along Ireland's western coast.

During their entire journey in the south and west of Ireland, the

Fosters were fully aware of the huge numbers wishing to escape from the hell all around them. Emigration, the last hope for many, spawned horrific stories associated with crammed coffin ships.

Often landlords, anxious to rid themselves of unwanted and wretched tenants, arranged for them to be transported in these ships. On board, the unfortunates found conditions abominable. Poverty, overcrowding, disease and filth were widespread; any food provided was mouldy and contaminated.

Frederick and Vere did not have sufficient time to investigate the stories of death from sickness and starvation, and of completely unseaworthy vessels which sank somewhere in the Atlantic with all occupants and crew lost. Later they would learn that of the 100,000 who chose to emigrate to North America in 1847, at least 20,000 were lost at sea, a staggering figure. The catastrophe of the supposedly seaworthy *Exmouth*, which came to grief on its passage from Derry to Quebec with a loss of 108 emigrants, was only one tragedy among many.

Having witnessed the atrocious conditions from which Irish peasants were struggling to escape, the Foster brothers made a momentous decision. They, themselves, would encourage emigration. The people had no chance to develop their potential as ordinary citizens, or even exist in Ireland, whereas other countries could provide the opportunity for them to enjoy fruitful and happy lives. Not only would the brothers encourage emigration, but they would provide financial assistance which, they agreed, must be disbursed under strict supervision.

For those poor families who could not or did not wish to emigrate, Frederick and Vere would provide the children with a basic schoolhouse education and the farmers with a sound grounding in modern methods of agriculture.

A religious blessing before departure

SIX

AGRICULTURE AND
'ASSISTED EMIGRATION'

FOLLOWING THEIR RETURN TO GLYDE COURT both Frederick and Vere Foster were physically and mentally exhausted. This, however, did not deter them from immediately pursuing some plans already in mind.

Frederick decided to take up permanent residence at Glyde Court. He was anxious to examine the needs and conditions of the tenantry there and in the surrounding area. Besides providing the people with maximum assistance he would devise schemes for promoting employment. Large numbers were at that time emigrating from County Louth due to lack of work and food.

Vere, ever convinced of the need for tenant farmers to receive some education in agriculture, decided to go to the Glasnevin Model Farm near Dublin. Opened in 1837, and later named Albert College, commemorating the Royal Visit to Ireland, it was established for the training of young farmers and prospective teachers of agriculture. (Such training was strongly advocated by the then Chief Secretary of Ireland, Lord Stanley, later Lord Devon.)

At the farm Vere met the Chief Agricultural Inspector, Dr Thomas Kirkpatrick, MD, who had a wide knowledge of such education in his native County Antrim. Vere informed the Inspector of his plan. Dr Kirkpatrick was impressed by the young aristocrat's desire to assist the Irish farming community in a practical way. He advised Vere that he should first enrol in the College's course in Agricultural Studies. Vere accepted and became a non-residential student. He obtained simple lodgings in the home of a Mrs Earl, near the farm.

Vere was still under thirty, with all the culture of Eton and Oxford behind him and the prospect of a glittering career before him. Yet he had, for all practical purposes, abandoned it, throwing himself instead into learning basic farming techniques. He was always magnanimous in everything demanded from him by his teachers and fellow-students, most of whom were ten years his junior.

Foster's eagerness to learn all he could was confirmed in the Inspector's comments in the 1850 Report of Commissioners of National Education in Ireland. In one passage, while drawing attention to the reluctance of some students to take part 'in the drudgery of agricultural labour', he singled out 'one of high rank' who did not fit into that category:

... but I need not go farther than our own day, our own country, and our own schools, to find an instance in which a gentleman of high acquirements, and independent fortune, (the brother of a baronet and High Sheriff of one of our eastern counties), in order to acquire a practical knowledge of agriculture, entered as an extern pupil at the Glasnevin establishment, and cheerfully assisted in all the farm operations. I have seen him with his coat off laying tiles in the bottom of a drain, and joining in every other kind of labour on the farm – yet he never thought it any degradation to be so employed, and I think it would be an insult to commonsense to ask whether he, or one of the same rank, who would be afraid to soil his fingers, should be entitled to the most respect ...[1]

Throughout this time Vere remembered his experiences in the famine-stricken districts of the country. Uppermost in his mind were the sufferings of the destitute poor subsisting on very little food and work.

Nowhere was this more in evidence than in the city of Cork. Many deaths were only prevented there due to the Society of Friends' Soup House. (Many other similar establishments were found throughout the country.) During their visit to Cork, the Fosters learned of the daily food distribution in the Barrack Street Depot to 1,300 poor. Tickets at one penny entitled each to a quart of soup with half a loaf of bread.

The Board of Public Works sometimes provided those in distress with employment on the building or repairing of roads, but normally the work was completely unnecessary and poorly paid. Indeed, many starving workers died before they had received their wages.

Vere Foster's expectations of the course at Glasnevin were that it would allow him to provide assistance for small farmers to obtain maximum results. But he found himself putting these plans aside, for two reasons. Firstly, he learned that the Society of Friends was at that time offering agricultural instruction while providing employment on a 500-acre farm at Ballina, County Mayo. The scheme was similar to what he had in mind and, according to reports, was successful. Secondly, he recognised the genuine desire of his fellow-students in Glasnevin to assist, whenever and wherever they could, small tenant farmers.

So, even though Vere was still undertaking his course in agriculture, he had come to definite conclusions regarding emigration. To remain in Ireland would mean death to tens of thousands, trapped in poverty and desperation. For these same people there was a new life, hope and plentiful employment in the United States and British North America (Canada). He preferred these territories because the sea journey was shorter than to Australia or New Zealand. In a memorandum on the issue he wrote:

> I believe that the most speedy and effectual PRESENT means of (assisting the victims of the Famine) is by personally aiding and advocating the emigration of a portion of the population to some other more favoured land.[2]

This marked the launch of Vere Foster's revolutionary scheme of 'assisted emigration' into which he threw himself and his fortune.

The year's course at Glasnevin had not finished when, having informed Frederick at Glyde Court of his plans, he personally arranged for the emigration of forty girls from Ardee and Tallanstown, in County Louth, to the United States. Because of Frederick's recent inquiries in the country and his personal knowledge of the families concerned, he was able to suggest the names of girls in dire poverty who would be suitable for Vere's project.

With regard to their selection, Vere decided he must satisfy himself that each young lady genuinely wished to emigrate for the purpose of finding work. He obtained from her local doctor, clergyman or other responsible person a favourable recommendation regarding the girl's good character. On receipt of this, he purchased food, cooking utensils, bedding and clothing for their sea journey. In addition, he gave them money for expenses until they found work. (With later groups he had different financial arrangements.) Travel costs were paid to the Shipping Agent and details on each of the forty migrants' tickets included the girl's name, age and the cost of her fare. Other information included the name of the Liverpool Agent and that of the ship and its date of sailing. The party of girls were then ready to leave the Ardee district for New York.

From those earliest days Foster was interested in encouraging the emigration of young women because, as he put it in his evidence to the Select Committee on Land Laws in Ireland in 1882,

> they are the least able to get themselves out, and because, as I say, they are generally the most liberal in sending home help to bring out their brothers and sisters, if they so wish to go.[3]

In this regard, therefore, Foster made only one request from each young emigrant: they must send back part of their savings in order to rescue others of their families in the same way. And this they did, for during the ensuing 14 years almost £1,000,000 annually was returned to Ireland.[4]

Vere was satisfied at the successful commencement of his 'assisted emigration scheme'. He crossed to Liverpool with his first forty emigrants and saw them safely on board the *Constellation*, docked there and ready to sail to New York.

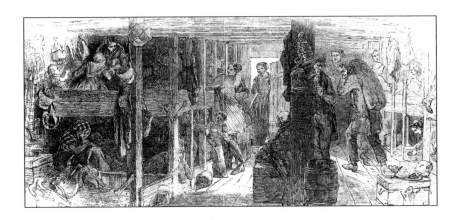

Between decks on an emigrant ship during the potato famine.

SEVEN

The Washington

A FLOATING HELL

VERE'S FEELINGS OF HAPPINESS were short-lived. He became quickly conscious of the fact that while he had spent much time attending to matters relating to the suitability of the forty emigrants, he had done relatively little to satisfy himself regarding their safe passage across the Atlantic or make forward arrangements for them in general. What would become of them during the sea voyage and arrival at New

York? These thoughts caused him much unease especially when he undertook an in-depth study of emigration.

He learned that besides the emigrants sent to Canada, the United States and the colonies by wealthy, charitable individuals, there were thousands emigrating who could afford their own fares. There were also large numbers who could scarcely find the wherewithal to leave, yet managed to do so by selling everything they owned. Yet another huge group consisted of families evicted from large estates in Ireland and Scotland. Many landlords felt, and the Earl of Mountcashel openly proclaimed, that 'the cost of maintaining a pauper for one year at home is as great as that of taking him out to the colony for which he may be intended and settling him there.'[1]

The arrangements made by such landlords for the transportation of 'paupers' were likely to be totally unsatisfactory. Many sought the cheapest shipping accommodation and food and made no provision for their emigrants after they reached their destination.

Sir James Matheson chartered a less than seaworthy vessel for £11,855 to clear the Scottish island of Lewis of 2,231 people. Lord Egremont and his son, Colonel Wyndham shifted 3,219 tenants from their estates in County Clare to Canada. 'I have seen something like a thousand passengers arrive from Lord Lansdowne's estate in Ireland', reported an official in Quebec in 1847. 'They had nothing; they had actually no shirts.'[2]

Foster could scarcely believe that Lord Palmerston, who had an estate at Mullaghmore, County Sligo, had 2,000 of his Irish tenants removed in nine vessels. The port authorities at Saint John, New Brunswick, were so shocked by the helpless and destitute state of Palmerston's tenants when his boat loads arrived for 'dumping' in Canada that an official complaint was made to the Lieutenant Governor of Canada.

Vere read Palmerston's 'explanations' in the House of Commons. His Lordship was unrepentant. As an absentee landlord he was 'informed' by his Irish land agents, Messrs Kincaid and Stewart, that all was the fault of the tenants themselves. They had requested from his agents on the Sligo estate passage, clothing and food for the journey, 'all of which was generously given'. However, the Canadian port official's report stated that 'most arrived in the most abject state of destitution with barely sufficient rags upon their persons to cover their nakedness ... one boy brought on deck stark naked'. Palmerston's agents argued that this was no fault of theirs but must have been caused by the 'exigencies of the voyage'.

Another Irish landlord who authorised such barbaric practices was the Hon. C.B. Wandesford who shipped almost 5,000 tenants from Kilkenny to North America.

Much of the information on emigration which Vere so urgently researched was registered in *Hansard*, the official record of Parliament. In 1847 Mr B. Hawes announced in the House of Commons that 90,000 emigrants had left for Canada. Of these 'no less than 15,000 died on board the vessels or immediately after landing'.[3] Hawes singled out a case on record of a ship full of Irish emigrants which reached New York with *sixty per cent of its passengers dead*. 'As she crawled up the Hudson River, between 30 and 40 bodies were lying on deck because, by then, no one had the strength to put them over the side.'[4]

This was happening as the Bishop of Limerick delivered a homily on pauper economy before a Select Committee of the House of Commons on emigration:

> 'Now, emigration', the Prelate observed, 'is an instantaneous relief. It is what bleeding would be to an apoplectic patient. The sufferers are at once taken away from a country where they are a nuisance and a pest to a country where they will be a benefit and a blessing.'[5]

While tens of thousands of Irish emigrants continued leaving from English ports, yet more were arriving, often crammed into the holds of coal vessels. 'There were so many of them', said the Hon. F. Scott in

Parliament in 1849, 'that a large emigration ship could easily be freight-ed with emigrants every two days.'[6]

Reports reaching Ireland from emigrants confirmed much of the information Vere was amassing at this time. These ranged from girl pas-sengers being flogged by crew members to passengers being starved of food. Often captains ordered food to be withheld, or it ran out when storms caused ships to arrive at their destinations anything up to four weeks late. These dreadful experiences were the lot of both emigrants who paid their own fares and those evicted by landlords.

There was no rigid Government inspection of emigrants' accommo-dation. Men, women and children were crammed on board wretched hulks. They died in their thousands from disease and malnutrition dur-ing the protracted sea journey. Those who survived the passage were often thrown friendless and penniless on the wharf of a port in North America, finding themselves little better off than they had been in Ireland.

A dreadful fact which emerged was that while thousands of emigrants were evicted to North America and the British colonies, no arrange-ments had been made to settle them on arrival. The emigrants were solely dependent on the charity of their new country to exist. Landlords and their agents usually deemed it unnecessary to accompa-ny groups of passengers to ensure both their safety at sea and work on arrival.

One notable exception came to light in Foster's investigations. He was Stephen de Vere, a nephew of Lord Monteagle. De Vere was not a landlord himself. However, on learning that some people in County Limerick were planning to emigrate to Canada, he decided not only to pay for their passages, but to accompany them and assist in finding them employment. Should he witness or experience any of the indig-nities which he heard emigrants were suffering at sea, he was deter-mined to have these exposed in Parliament. Indeed so great were the agonies of that journey to Quebec that de Vere, on his arrival there, opened a hostel for the many ill persons in his group. There, as he had done on the ship, he attended personally to their needs. He also provided accommodation in his hostel for those seeking employment.

In his Report to the House of Lords, 'immense mortality', 'extraordinary sufferings' and 'fetid infection' were among the phrases de Vere used to describe the conditions which he and his fellow steerage passengers had suffered. The Lords were shocked not only by what they heard but also by the fact that the maritime laws were so lax. They demanded improvements in passenger accommodation on emigrant ships and a general tightening up of the Passengers' Act.

Foster found it repugnant that Lord Palmerston, his own relation, could have been associated with the infliction of such cruelties on his Irish tenants during their sea voyages. His reading of Stephen de Vere's description of his dreadful personal experiences finally persuaded him to investigate the conditions on board emigrant ships for himself without delay.

On Sunday, 27 October 1850, accompanied by James Ward, a retired literary teacher at Glasnevin Model Farm, and clothed and equipped like the most wretched of the emigrants, Foster embarked incognito on the *Washington* at Liverpool. This 1,600 ton emigrant ship was one of the largest afloat and belonged to an American company, 'The Black Star Line'. Vere used a diary to record conditions during the voyage and thus accumulate evidence which would force the Board of Trade to introduce stringent legislation controlling the operation of emigrant ships.

Pages 2 and 3 of his diary include the following graphic details:

> All passengers who arrive at Liverpool a day or two before the sailing of an emigrant ship have to be inspected by a surgeon appointed by the Government, who will not allow anyone to go on board who has

an infectious disease of a dangerous character. I passed before him for inspection. He said without drawing breath, 'What's your name? Are you well? Hold out your tongue; all right' and then addressed himself to the next person ...

There was no regularity or decency observed with regard to taking the passengers on board ship; men and women were pulled in any side or end foremost like so many bundles. I was getting myself in as quickly and as dextrously as I could when I was laid hold of by the legs and pulled in, falling head foremost down upon the deck and the next man was pulled down on top of me ... The porters heap upon the passengers all kinds of filthy and blasphemous abuse, there being no police regulations, and the officers in the ship taking the lead in the ill-treatment of the passengers ...

The *Washington*, still anchored in the Mersey river, had no regular system for ensuring that each passenger received the daily allowance of water. Foster recorded the scene:

I witnessed the whole 900 and odd passengers called forward at once to receive their water. Its serving out was twice capriciously stopped by the mates of the ship who, during the whole time, without any provocation, cursed and abused, and kicked the passengers and their tin cans. Water was given to only 30 of the passengers, the remainder were made wait until the next morning. At the time of that incident I gently remonstrated with one of the mates who was cuffing and kicking the poor steerage passengers ... but he said he would knock me down if I said another word.

On 30 October 1850, the ship was well at sea yet no food whatever had been served out. The complaints of the poorer emigrants were naturally increasing as they had no means of existing except on the charity of other passengers who had brought some provisions with them for the anticipated six weeks' journey. At the time of this voyage and, indeed, until 1855, the law only required captains to provide supplementary food – passengers were expected to bring most of the provisions for the voyage themselves. Most of the emigrants were too poor to buy any additional food and relied solely on what was distributed during the voyage. Passengers, therefore, often arrived in Northern America suffering from near-starvation.

While aboard the *Washington,* Vere, aware of the passengers' growing anger, 'drew up a letter' to the captain of the ship, A. Page. In it, he informed the captain that 'it was three entire days since the ship sailed from Liverpool without our having received one particle of the stipulated provisions'. But the letter was never delivered for, as Foster tells us: '… while writing this at the request of my fellow passengers, the first mate, Mr Williams, knocked me down flat upon the deck with a blow in the face.' (Ten passengers added their signatures).

Vere's diary conveys the full horror of the emigrant's plight:

> Another day has elapsed without provisions being served out …
>
> It being wintertime it was impossible to read by daylight down below … I passed most of my time preparing soda-bread for myself and others and waiting my time in the cook-house where the weak and penniless were kept six or seven hours at a time attending the cook's pleasure or told with an oath that if they did not take their victuals as they were, i.e. half-cooked, they would be thrown overboard … All passengers swarmed with lice … The mates were a set of brutes. The second mate was reported to have been killed by the sailors the day after arrival in New York.

The ship's doctor's inhuman activities matched those of the other crew members:

> 17th November: The doctor informed everyone that 'there are a hundred cases of dysentery in the ship and they will all turn to cholera and I swear to God I'll not go amongst them. If they want medicines they

must come to me.'

19th November: ... The doctor has no right to charge for any medicines, but has, I am told, received a great deal of money on board in the same way. Those unable to pay him received little or no attention. This behaviour also applied to the cooks. Passengers who gave them money or other presents often received three or four meals daily. Those who had very little money, or refused to give it on principle, were given only one meal per day – if at all.

25th November: Another child, making about 12 in all, died from dysentery from want of proper, nourishing food and was thrown into the sea, sewn up, along with a great stone, in a cloth ...

30th November: The doctor came down with the first mate and, to display his authority, drew himself up and swelled himself out excessively tremendous, roaring out, 'Now then, clean and wash out your rooms everyone of you, God damn and blast your souls to Hell'.

2nd December: A beautiful day ... took a pilot on board.

To meet the wishes of many of the passengers, Vere penned a few lines to make a public complaint regarding their ill-treatment. It was signed by himself and 128 others on board:

We testify, as a warning to, and for the sake of future emigrants, that the passengers generally on board this noble ship the *Washington*, commanded by A. Page, have been treated in a brutal manner by its officers, and that we have not received one half of the quantity of provisions allowed by Act of Parliament and stipulated for by us in our contract tickets.

When very close to New York harbour on 3 December 1850 (the thirty-ninth day), Foster recorded that a few of the extremely ill passengers were taken ashore to a hospital on Staten Island. He, himself, did not foresee then that he too would be hospitalised, suffering from dysentery and ophthalmia immediately the ship docked. This latter illness was the result of his having been knocked unconscious by one of the mates when he tried to protect another passenger from a crew member during a brawl.

Vere lay critically ill in hospital for two months, the sickness almost ending his life. Mercifully, he recovered and was discharged, but the traces of that illness stayed with him for many years.

After his discharge from hospital, Vere sent a long letter to Frederick, describing the *Washington* voyage, using detailed information from his diary. Vere requested his brother to pass it on to their cousin, Lord Hobart at the Board of Trade. Hobart, himself a sympathetic observer of Irish affairs, brought the matter up in Parliament and had it published as a Blue Book in 1851.[7]

Members of Parliament took the matter up with the Emigration Officer in Liverpool. Predictably they found that, as was the case with almost all other American captains of emigrant ships, no complaints had been filed regarding the conduct of Captain Page on the ship's arrival at New York.

When the ship returned to Liverpool, Captain Page was challenged but denied all the allegations. In the absence of evidence it was impossible to take the matter any further under British law, for a British court had limited jurisdiction over acts done at sea on a foreign ship. Many expressed their regret that Foster and the other passengers had not registered their grievances in New York. As one historian notes:

> Though Foster had campaigned valiantly, and taken positive steps to reform practices on board emigrant ships, the political and legal climate was unhelpful. Famine emigrants continued to suffer at the hands of corrupt captains, owners and agents.[8]

Such was the tide of popular indignation that new Passenger Acts were passed in 1855 by the British Parliament and the American Congress. These stipulated increases in the amount and range of food for passengers during trans-Atlantic voyages. For the first time meat and a variety of vegetables were to be provided and passengers were supplied with enough food to last the entire voyage.

Vere Foster could feel that his labours had not been in vain. Whereas the requirements of earlier Passenger Acts had been largely ignored, this new legislation contributed greatly to the protection of emigrants and the improvement of conditions on board ships.

Fleeing Irish emigrants hoped for a better life in the New World.

EIGHT

VERE'S EFFORTS FOR EMPLOYMENT
AND TEMPERANCE

EVEN WHILE RECUPERATING IN NEW YORK, Vere continued to devote himself to the whole question of emigration. His experiences on the *Washington* cast a shadow over his plans to assist more Irish emigrants on the perilous journey to North America. He was bitterly disappointed to learn that many emigrants arriving off ships at New World ports were being subjected to conditions as bad, if not worse, than those he had witnessed before embarkation in Liverpool.

The dreadful lodging-houses along New York's dockside were packed with confused and disoriented passengers who had been the victims of runners and man-catchers. Foster himself, not yet fully recovered from his illness, was dragged to one of these obnoxious dwellings. Some days later, a friend discovered what had happened and removed him to a hospital bed.

The full scale of this exploitation was reported in the *Irish Farmers' Gazette* in 1852:

> On arriving here (New York) a number of 'boarding-house man-catchers' pounce upon the passengers, and hurry them off to their respective dens, where they charge them from one-half to one dollar a day, for a portion of a bed and bad food; ply them with drink and charge them double their agreement, under some pretence or other, and pretend to get them canal or railroad tickets at a discount, while all the while adding several dollars to the price, and then ask for a present for having protected them from being cheated ...[1]

Vere decided that all his future emigrants would be met immediately their ships berthed and taken to their places of employment. This would avoid their subjection to the cunning practices of villains at the ports of entry.[2] It was dreadful for Foster to hear many of these rogues at New York quay-side speak with Irish accents!

Vere needed to assure himself that there was indeed ample labour for the Irish in the United States. He was all too aware that thousands had arrived only to find themselves unemployed. Consequently, he approached a number of prospective employers in New York. He had in mind principally female domestic staff.

Initial contacts were very encouraging. Many employers expressed their willingness to receive young respectable domestics; they would receive good wages. Others promised to find employment for all willing workers in suitable homes. Each trusted Vere's assurance of the suitability and good character of the girls.

Armed with a letter of authentication from Lord Carlisle, the former Chief Secretary for Ireland, Vere set out to enlist the assistance of men of stamp in New York. In a letter to Foster, dated 6 October 1850, Carlisle wrote:

> I hardly need to trouble my American friends with direct letters of recommendation, but if you will mention to those whom I have named to you ... that you are a distant connection of mine, that from family, character and disposition you are well entitled to their consideration, and that you are anxious to make enquiries about the position and prospects of emigrants, I have no doubt you will find them ready to show you any attention which may be in their power.

The English peer recommended Vere to a series of public figures in New York and Washington, amongst them the British Consul, Anthony Bewley.[3]

From his initial approaches to these and other potential employers, Foster was confident in the soundness of his emigration scheme. In the first four months, he arranged employment for several hundred domestic staff and had every reason to believe more would follow. In order to improve the prospects for new emigrants, he circulated a printed questionnaire 'Information Wanted' among American employers seeking vital information on wage rates, the cost of lodgings and other important factors. So successful was the response that he followed it up with a much more detailed questionnaire two years later.

During his travels Foster wrote at least a dozen letters to his mother and Frederick with details of his work. Among the memorable visits he described was a night's stay at Grosse Isle, on the St Lawrence River, thirty miles from Quebec. Grosse Island was the quarantine station for that city. All contaminated ships with ailing passengers were required by

Canadian and US maritime law to fly a yellow flag and drop anchor at such a quarantine station on entering their territories. Ships were only allowed to proceed after their passengers had been adjudged well enough to travel to their port of entry. Other stations included Partridge Island (Canada) and Staten Island (New York).

Grosse Isle had witnessed shocking mortality during the worst year of the Great Famine. No one knows exactly how many people died there during the terrible summer of 1847, but Dr Douglas (the medical officer) spoke of 50 deaths a day at the height of the epidemic and recorded a total of 5,424 as being buried on the island. Many hundreds, perhaps thousands, died on board the ships before they ever reached Canada and their bodies were dropped overboard.[4]

At this time also, Vere despatched a long and informative letter to the *Irish Farmers' Gazette*. In it he detailed areas where work was available, the cost of living, price of land and subsidies, suitable crops and housing. He included reliable information on the construction of the Pennsylvania railroad, for which unskilled labourers, masons and stonecutters were needed. This was also the case for the Mobile to Chicago rail-link, for which wages were one dollar a day and boarding two dollars a week. Men were required for the Ohio Public Works and 'girls, even grumpy ones, but especially such as will make themselves agreeable will find permanent homes in a short time, with the greatest facility'. Vere stressed a further attraction for single women: 'they would have an extensive pick of husbands, unlike Limerick, which has 16,000 males and 28,000 female inhabitants'![5]

In his letter, Vere urged emigrants to leave the American seaports as soon as possible instead of 'lounging away their time, and sticking like glue in the large cities'. In particular, he hoped they would avoid 'spiritous liquors' and 'proclaim their aversion to the practice of drinking them' by following the advice of Fr Theobald Mathew, the Irish 'Apostle of Temperance', by taking the 'Total Abstinence Pledge' (which Vere himself had taken). It saddened Foster that great numbers of Irish men, by their drunken, riotous and quarrelsome behaviour and Irish girls by their slovenliness and dishonesty, were discrediting the Irish name among Americans who were thus reluctant to hire them. Employers had often told Vere that, apart from the one great failing of intoxication, they preferred Irish workers to Germans.

Vere first met Fr Mathew, a Capuchin friar from County Tipperary, renowned for his work in fighting drunkenness, at Louisville, Kentucky, in 1849. He was impressed to find that some 400,000 persons had signed the pledge since the friar's arrival in the United States. The great majority of those, Vere noted, stuck to it.

Vere was greatly honoured to meet the preacher for whom he had developed a profound admiration since his travels in Munster and Connacht. Fr Mathew's was already a household name amidst the squalor and poverty of Cork. Here, he had set up schools for various age groups, rented lofts where he had established industrial teaching – the girls being taught knitting and needlework and the boys various trades. Fr Mathew was ever in the thick of the work, constantly devising new experiments to raise the standards of the poor and dejected.

From his base, Fr Mathew travelled extensively throughout Ireland. In 1843 he toured Britain and later the United States. Vere was convinced there was much he could learn from the Irish friar and he hoped they could pool their ideas and resources to help people in need.

Following his return to Ireland, Vere made an early attempt to renew their acquaintance only to learn that Fr Mathew's exertions had undermined his health. In December 1856, the 'Apostle of Temperance' died and Vere joined a vast concourse of mourners at the funeral of the young Capuchin.

SIXTH EDITION—TWO HUNDRED AND EIGHTIETH THOUSAND.

WORK AND WAGES;

OR, THE

𝔓𝔢𝔫𝔫𝔶 𝔈𝔪𝔦𝔤𝔯𝔞𝔫𝔱'𝔰 𝔊𝔲𝔦𝔡𝔢

TO THE

United States and Canada,

FOR

FEMALE SERVANTS, LABORERS, MECHANICS, FARMERS, &c.

AS I WAS.   AS I AM.

Containing a short description of those countries, and most suitable places for Settlement; Rates of Wages, Board and Lodging, House Rent, Price of Land, Money matters, &c.; together with full information about the preparations necessary for the voyage, instructions on Landing, and expenses of Travelling in America. With Appendix, containing rates of Farm Laborers' Wages and Board in 88 districts.

BY VERE FOSTER.

LONDON:—W. & F. G. CASH, 5, BISHOPSGATE WITHOUT.

MANCHESTER, HEYWOODS; NORWICH, J. DARKEN; NEWCASTLE, BARKAS; LIVERPOOL, SHEPHERD; GLASGOW, GALLIE & SONS; EDINBURGH, MENZIES; DUBLIN, M'GLASHAN, MASON; YORK, J. BROWN; BRISTOL, W. H. COOK; BIRMINGHAM, WHITE & PIKE; IPSWICH, RIDLEY & GRIMWADE, DRUGGISTS; ABERDEEN, A. BROWN & Co.,

AND ALL BOOKSELLERS.

PRICE ONE PENNY EACH; OR TENPENCE PER DOZEN.

Vere Foster's Penny Emigrant's Guide, 1852

NINE

VERE'S ASSISTED
EMIGRATION PROGRAMME

Returning from his long visit to the New World late in 1851, Vere Foster was convinced that North America could provide a good livelihood for at least a million people. But how to transport such a number of penniless emigrants across the Atlantic Ocean? Aware of the many corrupt ship-owners, agents and captains involved in transporting migrants, Vere felt it was imperative to find a humanitarian shipping agent to assist him. One agent he felt he must meet was Henry Boyd of Liverpool. Foster had often heard Irish emigrants settled in the United States and Canada lavish praise on this particular agent for his kindness and care in arranging their passages with trustworthy ship-owners.

Vere met Boyd in Liverpool and was much impressed. The meeting resulted in an agreement that Henry Boyd would act as chief shipping agent in Liverpool for Vere Foster's future assisted emigrants. These he planned to select as soon as possible following his return to Ireland.

Before doing so, however, he visited his mother at her new home, 'Westcombe', Wimbledon, Surrey. Lady Albinia had only recently moved there, having lost heart in living at Branskea which she had sold to Colonel William Petrie Waugh for £13,000. To Vere's delight, his mother, who had become very interested in his work with emigrants, offered to place her home at his disposal. This was an offer Vere grate-fully accepted.

While at Wimbledon Vere wrote a follow-up booklet to his 'Emigrant's Guide'. It was entitled *Work and Wages* and was couched in simple language to help would-be emigrants to the New World. Foster was familiar with other publications for emigrants including *Practical Hints for Emigrants to Our Australian Colonies* by John Willox, *The Emigrant Voyager's Manual* by Willam H.G. Kingston and Scott and Jackson's *Openings for Gentleman's Sons on Farms, Ranches, Cattle Stations, etc Abroad.*

Through the easily accessible *Work and Wages* emigrants were able to gain important information about current rates of pay for various tradesmen and labourers, main travel routes, principal cities and other useful facts like suitable places to settle. Sold at one penny each (the price of a postage stamp), the booklet was revised five times and had a total circulation of 100,000. The final edition included illustrations contrasting the emigrant's poverty in Ireland with his prosperity in

America. It received a favourable review in *The New York Times* of 19 April 1855: 'the booklet helped in every way everything that can either be directly or even remotely useful to the artisan or the agricultural labourer ...'

The enormous response to this pamphlet was illustrated in a letter from Vere to Henry Boyd, dated 23 June 1854:

> I have received 926 applications by letter. (The first was from Philip Robarts, stone-mason, 2 Bankfield Terrace, Bootle, Lancs, England. Robarts enquired if one dollar would be sufficient to take him from England to Canada.) There have been between 3000 and 4000 verbal applications in London, 3000 in Glasgow, 1000 in Edinburgh, 1500 at Northampton, 1000 at Newcastle, 200 in Dublin, 2500 have been distributed in the villages about Norwich and there have been upwards of 1000 distributed in each of at least 30 other towns.[1]

Vere next informed Frederick of his future emigration plans. The two brothers were happy to be together again. Frederick decided to spend as much time as possible seeing to the affairs of his estates in County Louth. Vere, while not having a permanent address in Ireland, decided to open an office in Dublin. This swiftly became a hive of activity as applications began pouring in following the distribution of his *Work and Wages* pamphlets. Most applications were accompanied by appeals for assistance to emigrate. Vere began to realise the magnitude of the task he was undertaking. Again, he would need to satisfy himself of the character and working habits of each applicant. This information would be obtained from applicants' local police, clergy, teacher or other responsible persons but collating it would prove challenging.

The task of organising groups of emigrants to the United States and Canada, who varied in number between 20 and 150, was to strain Vere's financial resources. As the *Belfast Newsletter* later noted:

… it very often happened that those who were anxious to seek their fortunes across the Atlantic had not the wherewithal to pay even a portion of their passage money, and in these cases, when the honesty of the application was without doubt, Mr Foster paid the money himself.[2]

As with his first batch of emigrant girls from Ardee in 1850, Vere informed each emigrant that his or her passage expenses were only 'on loan'. To prevent them feeling they were going to America as paupers, he had certificates printed for each traveller, with the following characteristic admonition:

I expect you will repay the cost of your passage to America by sending for or otherwise assisting your relations in Ireland. If you have no occasion to do this, I hope you will send some money to me as a subscription to the Emigration Fund, to enable me to help a member of another family, selected like yourself on account of good character. I entreat you especially to love liberty and fair play for others as well as yourself, without distinction of race, religion or colour.[3]

The first to receive these certificates was a group of girls from County Clare. With sad yet hopeful hearts, they sailed to the United States in late 1852. Henry Boyd made their forwarding shipping arrangements at Liverpool. The Emigration Fund referred to on their certificates was the Irish Female Emigration Fund which Vere had founded earlier that year. Through it he wished to interest the general public in helping one able-bodied member of a family to emigrate to North America. In most cases a female would be specially selected on account of her poverty, good character and industrious habits in the expectation that she would take out other members of her family.

We see donations of one penny from a William Finerty and a Margaret Donaghy, as well as £5 and larger sums from wealthy people like Louise, Marchioness of Waterford and the seventh Earl of Shaftesbury. Vere, ever meticulous in his records of subscriptions received, was able to inform contributors in his Female Emigration Statement of July 1855, that he had collected £63 from 1050 persons.

On 12 April 1856, four years after the launch of the Female Emigration Fund (later known as the Irish Pioneer Emigration Fund), the *Dundalk Democrat* newspaper paid tribute to Foster's 'labours in promoting the emigration of poor females to Canada and the United States'. The writer continued:

> The philanthropy the worthy gentleman displays is creditable to his head and heart. He is spending his days in going about doing good. What a lesson to those who have means to assist the poor ...

In his Report on Female Emigration, Foster gave details of all money received and how it was expended. £550 was used to send 105 passengers to Quebec, New York, Charleston and New Orleans. Vere hoped that his kind subscribers would be satisfied that their financial aid had been judiciously applied. Moreover, it might encourage the promotion of similar emigration from other distressed districts, for instance from the Western Highlands of Scotland.

Vere was especially delighted at the number of emigrants who, having settled, had sent money or tickets back to their families in Ireland:

> I have recently visited the districts from which the emigrants were selected, and have ascertained the following facts most creditable to their industry and affectionate dispositions ... 71 have sent from America £756.10s, besides sending passage tickets for 21 persons. They have altogether been the means of taking out 86 additional persons.[4]

Among the list of names were Margaret Kelly from Feakle, County

Clare, who, besides sending home £24, also paid the passages for her brother Pat and three sisters; Catherine Collins, Feakle, sent £13 and arranged for two grown-up sons and two other children to receive passage tickets to America; three other female emigrants sent home amounts of £23, £27 and £26; Pat Moroney, from Feakle, sent £22 which took out his wife and four children from the workhouse; Michael Hagerty (Parteen), sent for two brothers, besides sending £8 to his mother; Pat Slattery (Bradford), sent £18, besides paying the passages of his wife and three children.

The Fosters' inspired choice of Henry Boyd as their agent was confirmed on receipt of letters from emigrants like those on board the *Garrick*, about to leave Liverpool on 2 July 1854:

Dear Sir,

According to your request we applied to Mr Boyd to put us in the best way of proceeding a ship to emigrate to America and we cannot leave England without acknowledging the kindness shown to us by that gentleman … One of our party was not ready to leave the country when we were, from Liverpool, so we went forward to procure passages for ourselves and him, but on his arrival in Liverpool he was accosted at the railway station by what is termed 'a runner', who by a volume of falsehoods made him believe that our ship had sailed. He then led him away to an office \and there parted with all the money he possessed to the runner who pretended it was for a ship to sail on 30th June. This was incorrect, as it was afterwards proved she was not to sail till the 6th July. But we are happy to say that by the exertions of Mr Boyd to the Emigrant Office the party who duped him was compelled to refund his money and he was allowed to take a berth on our ship.

Sir, we have cause to be truly thankful to you for sending us to a gentleman who so sympathises with emigrants … in your kindness direct emigrants to Mr Boyd, to whom too much praise cannot be given.

> Yours & C.
> H Chaplin & Family,
> George Hall & Do.
> From Hitchin, Herts., England

By the mid 1850s Vere was coming into possession of much solid information from North America as a result of his 'Information Wanted' circulars of 1852 and 1854 which provided the brothers with an accurate knowledge of work opportunities for their prospective emigrants. Horace Greeley of New York, (founder and editor of *The New York Tribune* and Democratic candidate for the US Presidency in 1872) suggested Virginia as the best area for emigrants in terms of agreeable climate, availability of work and cheap land. He urged emigrants to work for a farmer for one year to learn the ways of farming in that state.

Greeley emphasised the dangers of remaining in the cities. Thomas Boucher of Drury Creek, Illinois, an emigrant from County Clare, remarked that work for domestic servants and labourers was scarce in that state except on railroad construction, which was expected to continue for three years. William Chambers, (co-founder of *Chamber's Journal*) also strongly recommended that emigrants should not buy land on arrival but work for wages while learning the ways of the country. With regard to Florida, W.S. Dilworth, Monticello, warned that since so many African slaves were in domestic service, there would be no work in Florida for white emigrants.[5]

Armed with this up-to-date information on emigrant opportunities Vere made once or twice yearly trips to the United States and Canada, often accompanying emigrants to their destinations to ensure they obtained the employment arranged for them. He also wrote to the New Orleans newspaper *The Delta* on 22 April 1851 concerning the robberies and extortions experienced by Irish emigrants arriving there; he pleaded with the Irish settlers in New Orleans to help the new emigrants in every way possible, citing the successful work of the German Society formed to assist German emigrants in the United States.

During the latter half of the 1850s Vere met up with many groups whose emigration he had arranged. Normally they had settled into the employment and accommodation obtained beforehand; on other occasions, he found they had procured worthwhile work for themselves. In 1856, during a 7000 mile journey in the United States and Canada, he located 130 people for whom he had earlier arranged passages and work. These emigrants later organised the same service for 32 other family members. He also 'ascertained that one thousand and fifty eight pounds sterling had been remitted by 75 out of the 92 emigrants sent in 1852, and 97 additional persons had been sent for by them.'[6]

New York was the final centre Foster visited at the end of his journey. At that time, the city was already overcrowded with Irish emigrants, many of whom clung to its slum areas, often on the verge of starvation, unemployed and unemployable. Vere was learning that numerous Irish emigrants arrived in the New World with a complete lack of education and often illiterate. He felt more and more that this problem must be addressed at its source without delay.

The fact that an important, well-connected English gentleman was constantly working unobtrusively in North America for the poor of Ireland in their time of distress did not go unnoticed by leading Americans. One such person was the Catholic Archbishop of New York, Most Rev John Joseph Hughes. The Hughes family had themselves emigrated to the United States from Annaloghlan in the Clogher Valley of County Tyrone. (The home they left has been reconstructed in the Ulster-American Folk Park, Omagh.)

Archbishop Hughes had no hesitation in providing Vere with a letter of introduction when they met in August 1856. That letter was to prove of immense value to Foster in his later work with emigrants, both in the United States and Ireland. The Archbishop wrote:

Mr Foster, the bearer of this letter has been introduced to me under auspices highly honourable to himself and to the case in which he is engaged. That cause is philanthropic, and has a reference to the emigration of poor persons.

As he desires to consult Catholic clergymen and others in the United States on this subject, I beg leave to recommend him to the kind attention of such Catholic clergymen as he may have reason to call on.

+John Hughes
Archbishop of New York.[7]

The Archbishop's letter and the earlier one of Lord Carlisle enabled Vere to make many contacts and meet requests for girls of good character from Ireland, suitable for domestic service. Consequently while returning home in 1856, his time on board ship was almost completely taken up with preparing plans for the emigration of three hundred young people, mostly girls. The first group set out from Drogheda, County Louth three months after his return and was described in *The Drogheda Argus* of 19 December 1856:

On Monday morning Vere Foster, Esq left Ardee with about seventy female emigrants for Canada. About twenty of them had been inmates of the Ardee Union Workhouse, the remainder were from the town and surrounding country. They were all decently and comfortably clad, [the footwear and clothes being provided by Vere's mother. She knit all their socks herself]. The procession, consisting of an omnibus and eight or ten carts, moved along the road, with the worthy gentleman mounted on a common dray (horse) among his *protégées* ...[8]

On their arrival in Canada he set out with the group of girls to the various places of employment he had arranged for them. Vere had become well known to farm owners and others across Canada and the United States. They admired him for his selflessness and generous efforts to obtain employment for parties of poor and needy emigrants; they were glad to have him in their neighbourhoods where 'his genial and kindly presence, courtly manners and kind nature made him a welcome and interesting guest'. Commodious barns were often placed at his disposal as comfortable resting places for those he was accompanying.

Vere had many rewarding experiences while arranging employment. One was when he made the acquaintance of Abraham Lincoln, the future President of the United States, but then a country lawyer who encouraged him in his work with emigrants. (In a letter dated 26 April 1865, to the editor of the *Irish Times* following the murder of Lincoln, Foster recalled the kindness of both Mr and Mrs Lincoln in providing accommodation for himself and temporary work for one of the women whom he was moving west from New York in 1857.)

During that journey, Vere received a letter from his brother on the general situation in Ireland. Frederick felt that, as the economic situation was now improving, Vere should suspend his work on emigration. In its place, perhaps, he might consider helping in the recruitment of men for the Army in India following the Indian mutiny of 1858. It was also his wish that Vere should continue his efforts to improve schoolhouses in Ireland.

Sadly, this affectionate letter, along with its suggestions, was the last Vere would receive from his brother. Frederick died on 27 September 1857 at their mother's home and one month passed before Vere received word of it. He was heartbroken: not only had Freddie and he been true friends all their lives, but during these last years they had worked closely together on projects close to their hearts.

Vere knew it was Freddie's hope to settle in Ireland among the tenants he loved. The respect and affection in which he was held by his grateful tenants was reflected in the monument erected in 1861 in the centre of Ardee at a cost of £290, defrayed by their pittances. On the large statue of a Victorian gentleman and small fountain which still stand today in the Louth village, are inscribed the words:

TO THE MEMORY OF

SIR FREDERICK GEORGE JOHN FOSTER, BARONET

Erected by his Tenants

A.D. 1861

Following Frederick's death Vere visited his mother and his only surviving brother, Cavendish, living in his rectory in Essex where his parish duties were light. Now, the third Baronet Cavendish would become a wealthy man when Frederick's affairs were settled. Cavendish had also become a leading member of the evangelical branch of the Church of England.

Vere had never enjoyed the same warm relationship with Cavendish as he had with Freddie and their letters and conversations confirm this. Shortly after learning of Frederick's death Vere wrote to Cavendish on 6 August 1858 asking him to consider settling in County Louth with his family:

> ... What a great pleasure it would be to yourself and the children to be occupied in attending to the condition of the poor on the property who naturally look to you for employment, encouragement and assistance. A new school-house and teacher are wanted at Rathgar and more new cottages here and there. Do not distribute Bibles or Protestant tracts, or you will injure your power for good; proselytism is very odious ... I hope the children will be brought up in association with, and to feel an interest in the people on the property ...[9]

Relationships did not really improve, nor did Rev Cavendish settle permanently in County Louth or assist in the work of emigration.

However, after a further plea from Vere, he agreed to donate a site at Philipstown for a new school though Vere undertook to pay all the necessary costs.

Vere, however, did not desire to abandon his work for emigrants though he found himself confronted with unexpected hostility against a backcloth of religious proselytism and the demands of the 'strong farmers' for farmhands. These factors were apparent on 19 December 1856 on his arrival at Drogheda quay with the seventy emigrants bound for Canada. Vere would later recall the anger of the assembled crowds:

> ... Many of the farmers were mad with me for reducing the supply of labourers and servant girls; and alternate entreaties, threats and force were used to prevent many of my party from embarking, cries being got up that my intention was to make Protestants of them, that they were to be bound for a term of years, to be sold to the 'blacks', to the Mormons, etc, etc ...[10]

Later, someone in the crowd shouted that a girl among his group, Eliza Adams, was a 'souper', that is she had abandoned the Catholic faith for a bowl of soup. Such inducements had been employed throughout Ireland by certain unscrupulous clergymen during the Famine years. Vere was already aware of her 'conversion' because members of her new religion were requesting him to arrange her passage to Canada and paying her fare. Eliza would sail only to Liverpool with the party, then continue her journey onwards in another ship. While some of the adults were shouting that Vere intended using Eliza to proselytise the remainder of the group, others were searching her pockets and they discovered them filled with hundreds of tracts. These they angrily threw up in the air. Foster later acknowledged that a cold fear griped him on this occasion and 'he felt he just narrowly escaped execution ...'[11] The fact was, that as he had earlier told Cavendish, proselytism in any form was utterly repugnant to Vere.

Vere became aware of further feelings of disquiet among many in Ireland regarding emigration. These included landowners who were finding it difficult to obtain cheap labour which had once been plentiful. Some clergy argued forcefully that it was responsible for their parishioners' numbers falling; others thought that with the passing of the horrendous famine years, there was no longer any necessity for large-scale emigration. But Vere knew that people were continuing to leave Ireland on a massive scale and made the necessary arrangements for yet another group. The applicants left Ireland for Liverpool where they boarded the *City of Mobile* for New York. It was a journey that would cause Vere much anguish.

This time he did not accompany his charges but travelled ahead to the United States in a faster vessel. This had called at Queenstown, County Cork, enabling Vere to finalise plans for their employment, mostly as domestic staff. Immediately after the *City of Mobile* docked at New York he was deeply vexed to learn that some of the girls had disregarded his advice, allowing themselves to be abused by members of the ship's crew *en route*.

The incident received much adverse publicity in the New York newspapers. On their arrival at port the twenty young women were smuggled to the city's Water Street vice dens, declaring publicly that they refused to remain any longer under Foster's care. One newspaper, the *Irish Vindicator*, of 14 August 1857 proclaimed: 'VERE FOSTER'S EMIGRATION SCHEME MUST BE ABANDONED FORTHWITH.'

What a cruel stroke of fate it was that these malpractices, widespread on other emigrant ships, should have become linked, even remotely, with Vere Foster who had done so much to safeguard all emigrants from becoming involved in such depravity.

Having worked tirelessly to obtain information on the whereabouts of each girl, Vere returned to Ireland where he hurriedly issued a handbill to counter the adverse publicity the *Mobile* episode had generated there. This informed many angry parents that, although employment had been arranged for all the girls, some did not accept it and remained in New York against his wishes. Vere named the ninety-four girls whom he confirmed as having been safely delivered to their destinations, along with the addresses of those clergymen in whose care they were placed.[12] He intimated that, as he had many further applications for assisted emigration, he would attend to them and arrange for one hundred to travel to North America during the following month, September 1857. He was as good as his word.

Vere continued with his scheme of assisted emigration. But it came to an end with the outbreak of the American Civil War in 1861. He felt it was too dangerous to land people in a country ravaged by conflict. Yet Vere realised that these changed circumstances would provide him with an opportunity to respond to a new challenge. Over the next few years, he would devote his energies to the crying need for a better system of education in Ireland.

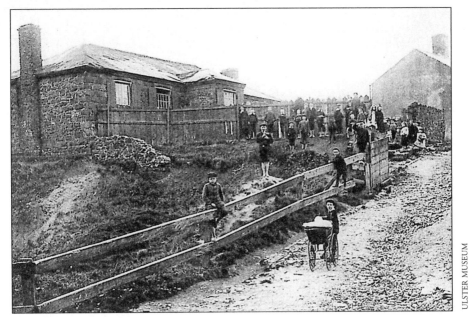

Squalor and overcrowding were the hallmarks of
Springfield National School, Belfast 1902

TEN

TRANSFORMING THE
NATIONAL SCHOOLS

VERE WAS ONLY THIRTY NINE YEARS of age when his selfless
enthusiasm to help the people of Ireland once again changed the
course of his life. Having completed a rigorous examination of Ireland's
educational system over the previous sixty years, he became convinced
that the improvement of National Schools and schoolhouses must now
be his first priority.

At the beginning of the 1800s, there were many schools involved in popular education. Those with a Protestant bias included the Charter Schools, the London Hibernian Society Schools, the Schools of the Association Incorporated for Discountenancing Vice and Promoting the Knowledge and Practice of Christian Religion, and those Schools of the London Baptist Society. Proselytism was the declared aim of the Baptist Society which used the Irish language as the teaching medium in its 86 schools, scattered throughout Connacht.

The final category, and by far the largest, comprised the Catholic-controlled schools. Sometimes known as 'hedge schools' or 'pay schools', these were attended by Catholic boys and girls and had Catholic teachers. Such schools had been banned under the Penal Laws but these statutes had lapsed by the late eighteenth century and many 'poor scholars' received a sound education at the hedge schools. Amongst these were William Carleton, the novelist of the Clogher Valley and Rev Dr Henry Cooke, the prominent Presbyterian who attended Joseph Pollock's hedge school near Maghera, County Derry. For a modest payment of about half-a-crown (12 1/2 p) per quarter from each pupil, they were taught a variety of subjects, with an emphasis on reading, writing and arithmetic – sometimes to a high degree. Itinerant hedge school teachers often taught Classics, especially in County Kerry, preparing young adults for the Irish Colleges in Paris, Rome or Salamanca, where many studied for the priesthood.

Hedge schools were usually sod or stone huts, or converted cattle sheds in the Irish countryside. Their ram-shackle appearance, with openings in the walls for doors and windows, reflected the poverty of the Catholic countryfolk in the wake of the penal era. The poorest pupils usually paid the 'Master' in kind, supplying him with turf or fowl. When the weather permitted, lessons were often held under a tree or in the shelter of a hedge.

Pat Frayne was a hedge schoolmaster in the townland of Skelgy,

County Tyrone. He had a daily attendance of nearly 100 boys and girls. According to Carleton, who was one of his pupils, 'a school-house was built for him – a sod house scooped out of the roadside – and in the course of a month it was filled with upwards of a hundred scholars …' Carleton recalled:

> Every winter's day each scholar brought two sods of turf for the fire which was kept burning in the centre of the one roomed school. There was a hole in the roof that discharged the functions of a chimney. Around this fire especially during cold and severe weather, the children were entitled to sit in a circle by turns … The seats about the fire were round stones.[1]

Writing of his Irish-speaking tenants in County Sligo in 1808, Lord Palmerston noted:

> The thirst for education is so great that there are now three or four schools on the estate … The people join in engaging some itinerant masters; they run him up a miserable hut on the roadside … They are taught reading, writing and arithmetic, and what, from the appearance of the establishment, no one would imagine, Latin and even Greek.

This situation was to change in 1831 with the establishment of the National Board of Education when a Government grant of £30,000 was provided for 'The Education of the Poor in Ireland'. At the same time the majority of the country's 10,000 schools (the former hedge schools) were given the title 'National Schools'.

All National Schools would now be vested in the Board, have Protestant and Catholic teachers, and be attended by both Catholic and Protestant children. Each would have a patron or manager – usually the local minister or parish priest – who would ensure that all children received their education in general subjects. Religious instruction would be provided in each National School, but outside school hours, by the respective clergymen or their appointees.

In the spirit of the time central government was to be seen aiding local initiative. Managers and parents would be responsible for providing sites for the building of schools, along with one third of the building costs and of teachers' salaries.

The government's wish that National Schools should be fully non-denominational was not to be realised, however. Some prominent Protestant Church figures, led by Rev Henry Cooke, DD, were emphatic in their opposition to the non-denominational principle. He won support for the view that Bible Reading and Religious Instruction (which the Board wanted to be extra-curricular) should be integral components of the curriculum. By 1840, Cooke's campaign was successful. The result was the Stopford Rule of 1847, by which National Schools became denominational. All the Protestant Churches came in fully behind the National Board of Education's offer, becoming vested and receiving grants.

The Catholic Church, for its part, largely accepted the national system from its introduction and the Archbishop of Dublin, Daniel Murray became a member of the Board. In the north, Archbishop William Crolly of Armagh, himself a product of a 'mixed school' in Downpatrick, was strongly supportive of the new system while Archbishop John McHale of Tuam condemned it as incompatible with the Catholic faith and refused to allow national schools in his archdiocese. His view was shared by the Irish Christian Brothers who withdrew from the system in 1836. Thus, many Catholic schools, especially in Connacht, were non-vested to the mid-1800s. As a result, they received almost nothing by way of grants; their school-houses and classroom furniture remained miserable and their teachers were poorly-trained and badly-paid.[2]

In 1840, the Board offered grant-aid to a Presbyterian school at

Correen, County Antrim, which refused the right of clergy of other denominations to enter the premises to impart religious instruction.

Any hesitation among the Protestant Churches towards establishing national schools in Ireland now evaporated. Their activities tended, unfortunately, only to confirm Catholic fears regarding the aims of certain evangelical societies. One such group, 'The Irish Church Mission to Roman Catholics', arrived in 1849 from England and opened relatively well-equipped schools in disadvantaged districts of Dublin and elsewhere. In these schools, according to the Report of the Commissioners of National Education for 1863:

> The teachers would feed and caress the children, distribute among them coal in the winter, dress them for the school, and teach them daily that the doctrines of the Roman Catholic Church are not the word of God – for what the priest teaches, Christ did *not* teach; the pupils learn anti-Catholic hymns, and join in anti-Catholic prayers.[3]

Proselytism had indeed reappeared in Irish education.

In 1858 Vere made a lightning tour of schools in his ancestral County Louth. Forced to 'overnight' in draughty inns, he missed the creature comforts of Glyde Court: 'I shall be glad to get back to a dry and solitary bed after so long, a sleepless experience of damp and crowded beds – crowded with bugs and fleas enough to serve as snuff ...'. He did so, ever-conscious of his late brother's desire, repeated in his last letter, to assist Irish education, but was shocked to see the ninety eight hovels which served as schools. Most were without privies, school furniture, maps, apparatus or fireplaces; often the children had to sit on damp earthen floors. Vere made immediate contact with the Commissioners of Education and offered to defray one third of the building costs of twenty new, high-quality schools, which he felt were desperately needed in the county. In addition, he would pay the total cost of erecting teachers' houses near each school. The entire building project was to be vested in the Board.

The offer was a very generous one but, to Vere's bitter disappointment, it was turned down. The Catholic Church informed the Board that it was unwilling to take advantage of Foster's offer because of the latter's request that the school-houses and teachers' dwellings be vested. The Board, in turn, informed Vere that it could have no further interest in his proposal: it had wanted the proposed school-houses – which would have been attended almost exclusively by Catholic children – to be under its jurisdiction. The Hierarchy, however, was urging the Irish Christian Brothers and other teaching Orders to manage the new schools.

Although Vere was unable to do anything about these differences between the Board of Education and the Catholic Church, he still yearned to improve the ramshackle schools, vested or non-vested, in the county. Indeed, when he left Ardee and travelled the highways and byways of the country, he soon discovered that vested schools were in an equally poor state of disrepair. The problem was that many schools did not receive the necessary funding for their maintenance and efficiency.

Increasingly, Foster became convinced that each vested school should have definite and sustained incomes from three sources: government grants, local taxation and voluntary donations from local landlords. He had no compunction in making his thoughts known on the pitiably inadequate contributions made by landlords towards the building and upkeep of their local school-houses. He stoked controversy by publishing a list of titled gentry in the west of Ireland who had almost 1,300 National Schools on their properties. In his view they were guilty of gross negligence towards their tenants:

> Twenty-eight well known Noblemen with sixty-five National Schools contributed only a miserable £51. ... 240 other National Schools on

the properties of six Marquises, fourteen Lords, twenty-nine Baronets and six Knights, receive no contributions whatever from their land-lords who are, of course, mostly absentees ... One would expect that they would be the most liberal promoters of the education of the children of the labourers and tenants on their estates, the sweat of whose brows is the foundation of their wealth.[4]

Vere now had experience of all types of school from his investigations throughout the country. During his journeys, he had three main objectives. The first was to obtain from the school teachers testimonials, references or credentials for prospective local emigrants. Another was to locate people in the area to whom he had been asked to deliver letters or messages from people he had met in the United State and Canada. A third aim was to view the state of the local schoolhouses at first-hand.

From the outset Vere involved himself in deciding what improvements were necessary to the school-houses and in ensuring that these were carried out. The majority had thatched roofs which allowed rain and snow to enter, while the floors were earthen, damp, dirty and uneven. Invariably, the schools were crammed with children dispatched by their parents as much for heat as for education. Vere would often quietly note the measurements of the classroom with his walking stick. Later he would arrange for workmen to visit each school. They replaced the earthen floors with wooden ones and the thatched roofs with slates while they mended the windows and made the necessary repairs. School apparatus, desks and the like often arrived shortly afterwards.

Foster had the work carried out entirely at his own expense and it was unknown for him to refuse any school he found in need of repair. When he felt there was sufficient local money available he requested that at least some of the repair or building expenses be defrayed by the school authorities. On other occasions he made donations to schools for specific purposes. One example was Shivdelagh National School,

Country Leitrim to which he donated £5 on 30 April 1859, suggesting, too, how it should be spent.

During his lifetime, even when he was involved in other major philanthrophic work, Vere improved some 2,000 school-houses in this way, or built new ones at his own expense. All grants, whether towards the initial cost of building or towards their improvement, were given unconditionally. This was in stark contrast to the rigid demands which the Board of National Education attached to any monies which it allocated.

Foster's generosity was keenly appreciated by children and teachers in receipt of his help and they continually expressed their thanks in poems and letters. Typical was the following tribute in verse sent to Vere by the teacher and pupils of Killycarvan National School, County Monaghan, dated 24 January 1861:

> The pupils so happy, one school-house so neat
> Our floor is now boarded, it looks so complete,
> Do thank most sincerely that man of great fame,
> That lover of science, 'Vere Foster' by name,
> For his princely donation, unsolicited given,
> We can only thank, his reward is in heaven.
>
> To the emigrant lonely he has been a guide,
> To watch o'er the poor is his pleasure and pride,
> To aid, to improve and to better their lot,
> Abroad on the ocean, or at home in their cot,
> His princely donation so freely he's given,
> We can only thank – his reward is in heaven.[5]

From the Irish-speaking village of Belmullet in County Mayo, which had suffered greatly during the Famine, the local teacher, Martin Walsh, addressed Vere in terms of admiration in 1859:

Your Honour will, we trust, be pleased to accept our hearty thanks for your kind and valuable Gift, the School Apparatus ... suspended on the walls of our room made so very comfortable at your expense.

Praise coming from so humble a source in this remote part of Ireland can be of small consequence to you who are so highly applauded by all who know how to appreciate real worth, but it is the only way we have in our power at present to acknowledge our Gratitude ...[6]

One day in April 1863 a bulky envelope arrived at Vere's little Belfast office. In it was a letter to which was attached the signatures of one hundred teachers in County Longford, expressing their 'gratitude and veneration' for his 'active benevolence':

You sought us in our dwellings and were not discouraged by the contact; you stood by us in our schools and showed your appreciation of our labours by those generous gifts of educational apparatus hitherto unfortunately beyond our reach ... Startled by the suffering of the half-clad children, you substituted for the damp, unwholesome clay, the dry boarded floor, and in other important respects, exerted yourself for the promotion of decency (privies), cleanliness and order in our schools.[7]

Vere never avoided the cold winter weather when moving on foot across the country. It has been estimated that he visited some 1,400 schoolhouses between 1859 and 1863. The 1870 edition of the *Irish Teachers' Journal* reported that in that year alone, Foster spent £13,000 on school repairs and classroom apparatus.

Such generosity did not go unnoticed by schools inspectors and influential people in the field of education. Even the Lord Lieutenant, in 1859, was informed of Vere's donation of £2,142.8s.10d. to school repairs and equipment in 785 needy cases. The Report of the Commissioners referred to:

... the unexpected co-operation of a gentleman (Vere Foster Esq.) who previously had, I believe, not the slightest connection with the schools of the district, or the estates on which they are situated. With princely, but discriminating generosity, he has given sums of money, often very considerable, for effecting the most useful improvements in the school-houses ...[8]

The Report contrasted Vere's vision and generosity with that of many public figures:

As a grand contrast to the indifference of so many to the progress of popular education, it gives me sincere pleasure to mention the noble efforts in this district of a gentleman ..., I allude to Mr Vere Foster, whose active benevolence was a few years since, successively devoted to the welfare of the poor emigrant, and his name identified with the protection of female purity, is as a household word in the cottages of the people. This gentleman has ... opened a correspondence with upwards of 4,000 teachers explaining his plan and inviting local co-operation ... It would appear that, with him, the knowledge of a national defect is the precursor to the adoption of a remedy.[9]

Vere was searching for just such a remedy. Already shocked by the shameful conditions of Irish schools, he was equally dismayed by the low standards of teaching in many of them. More and more his sympathies began to lie with undervalued teachers who, besides practising their craft in hovels, were forced to teach without proper resources or facilities.

His next major goal, he averred, must be the improvement of teaching standards across Ireland.

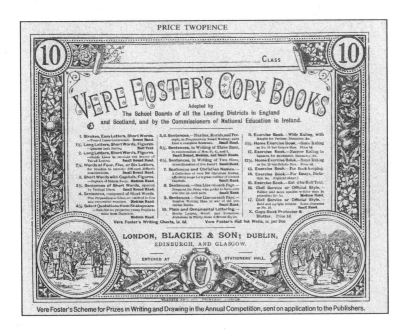

VERE FOSTER'S COPY BOOKS

Adopted by
The School Boards of all the Leading Districts in England
and Scotland, and by the Commissioners of National Education in Ireland.

LONDON, BLACKIE & SON; DUBLIN,
EDINBURGH, AND GLASGOW.

ENTERED AT STATIONERS' HALL.

Vere Foster's Scheme for Prizes in Writing and Drawing in the Annual Competition, sent on application to the Publishers.

ELEVEN

VERE FOSTER'S
FAMOUS COPY BOOKS

Vere found that the misery he had experienced in the National school-houses was indeed matched by an extremely low standard of education in them. This was confirmed by the National Board of Education Report of 1841:

It was found that of all the population over five years of age, 53 per cent were illiterate, 19 per cent were able to read but not write [while] 28 per cent were able to read and write.

Many people in Ireland were thus forced to pay neighbours and friends to write letters for them or to read the few letters they received. The following would have closely resembled the kind of letters which Vere himself often brought to the families concerned and read to them:

> Dear Mother I Rite these fuee lines to you hoping To find you in good health As this Leaves Me at present I thank god for it Dear Mother we were foure weeks at say and we got a fone passage God favoured me I never was one Day sick I thank God for it … Dear Mother the day we landed in St Jonhs New Brunswick my sister Marget left and went to Boston my Sister Elon went after her to Boston and I got no Account from them since I parted her Dear Mother I am getting along here and getting good health I thank God for it …
>
> Direct your letter to Agusta State of Maine. One Boyle One (Eoin) Boyle, Augusta, Maine.[1]

> Dear Father and Mother, I taake the present opportunity of letting you know that I am in good health hoping that this will find you and all friends the same … here were 4 Deaths on the passage but the second day after we arrived here and after the Doctor came on Board the Sickness commenced. My dear little Biddy died. Dear Father Pen could not write the distress of the Irish Passengers which arrived here thro Sickness death and distress of every Kind … Here are thousands of theem buried in the Island and those who could not go to the States are in the Poorhouse or are begging thro the streets of St John … I think times will mend here after some time and dear Father I will soon send you some help. No more at Present but I remain your affectionate Daughter till Death

Catherine Hennigan
St John, New Brunswick
15 February 1848. [2]

Having seen for himself the lack of educational facilities and teachers struggling to teach against impossible odds, Vere understood very well why this state of affairs existed.

Teachers often had no classroom furniture, blackboards, chalk or other writing or reading material; neither were there any slates, chalk or other writing and reading material for the children. Vere witnessed children walking barefoot two or three miles daily to and from their school, each carrying a heavy slate tied around his neck. For one who loved children this was a distressing sight and Foster continued to search for a remedy.

Some writing aids were available for schools that could afford to pay for them. These included 'Dollier's Copy Books', 'Johnston's Upright Copy Books' and the almost useless 'Headline' cardboard strips. (The latter deteriorated quickly with use.) Vere approached the Commissioners of National Education to have more suitable books produced, but failed to persuade them. Teachers were left to make do with their meagre supply of reading and writing material, which seldom changed. As a result, penmanship and reading were generally neglected.

The memory of Lord Palmerston, now Prime Minister of the United Kingdom, often came to Vere's mind while wondering how he could help to provide children with a more effective method of acquiring basic writing skills during their elementary education. He recalled his time with Palmerston in the Foreign Office and, in particular, the Minister's circular to members of staff that they must write in copperplate. Vere decided to seek an appointment with the Prime Minister, inform him of his desire to improve writing in Irish schools, and seek his advice. Palmerston admired Foster's motives and enthusiasm in this field and made a number of suggestions. These were that Vere should make a study of the writing and copy books then in use and then design a set himself. Both agreed that this new set should not resemble any in use in Ireland at that time but rather should aim at helping girls and boys to find remunerative employment.

Now forty years of age, Vere tackled this challenge with an enthusiasm that matched all his earlier ventures. He made a series of trips to European countries and the United States where he examined the most popular forms of writing systems in their schools. Having chosen what he considered were the best example in each, he returned to Ireland where he discussed them with some of the inspectorate and most competent teachers. Even though he often suffered from bouts of chronic illness resulting from the *Washington* voyage, he continued with this rewarding work. During this period prayers were offered throughout Ireland for his return to good health.

Despite these problems, Vere Foster's first and unique Head-line Copy Books appeared in 1865. They would revolutionise the teaching of penmanship, not only in Ireland but throughout the English-speaking world. Specially engraved copper plates were used in their preparation and the paper was of excellent quality. The first edition of the Copy Books was printed by Forster & Co., Crow Street, Dublin, in the Machinery Department of the Dublin Exhibition and the publishers were D W Carroll, Dublin and Whittaker & Co, London. All initial costs were paid entirely by Foster.

Once satisfied with this first set of thirteen books, Vere forwarded it to the Prime Minister who made minor amendments here and there. It gave him much pleasure to write on 28 January 1882, seventeen years later: 'I still have in my possession the first proofs, revised in the handwriting of the Prime Minister himself.'[3] As a token of thanks and appreciation, the title given them on their semi-stiff covers was 'The Palmerston Series'. Within a few years that title was changed to 'VERE

FOSTER NATIONAL SCHOOLS COPY BOOKS'.

Conscious of the need to win the goodwill of the National Board, Vere despatched the proposed first series to them in manuscript form. Board Members agreed to allow it to be used for a trial period and ordered 50,000 copies at £6.4s.0d (£6.20) per thousand. Foster had intimated that this price was half that involved in their publication and that each copy-book could therefore sold in schools at one penny (or in some cases a half-penny) – within the reach of the poorest child. The Board was also acquainted with the aims of the copy-books which were four-fold – the teaching of legible, standard writing, spelling, thinking and character formation.

There was a huge and immediate demand, something which had not been anticipated. Approximately one million of the 8 x 6 inch copy-books were sold in their first year alone and soon they had replaced the older, inferior primers. Schools throughout Ireland became familiar with the motto printed on the attractive cover of each Copy Book: 'A Nation's greatness depends upon the education of its people'. Soon afterwards, the cover bore the imprimatur: 'Adopted by the Commissioners of National Education in Ireland'.

The first book followed a distinct pattern. It commenced with pen strokes, then letters of the alphabet followed by short and simple words. Book Number 8 introduced short sentences, each with a proverb. All thirteen books in the first series had the strokes and sentences written along the top line of each page. Children then copied these on to the lines provided below. (Some had vertical lines on the pages to help children copy each word exactly into its correct space.)

Sales continued to rise as different book titles were introduced. Children, and teachers particularly, loved those which contained proverbs: 'A stitch in time saves nine', 'Great barkers seldom bite', 'Idle people never prosper', and 'Extravagance ruins many a family'. Then there were books with sentences introducing Christian names, various kinds of hand including 'Large Round Hand'; 'Half Text Hand'; 'Ladies' Finishing Hand'; 'Plain and Ornamental Writing' and Home Exercise books. Copy Book Number 10 introduced the student to French, German and Celtic lettering with '*Cead Mile Failte*' prominently displayed.

On the inside of the earliest copy books was valuable information for teachers on how to assist children to write properly and keep their work tidy, as well as the use of blotting paper. In addition, Vere emphasised the use of proper pens and nibs, good quality ink, oval-shaped Hat Ink wells (shaped and to his own design) at 7 pence per dozen and Vere Foster pencils at 4s.3d. a gross.

Copy books for older children provided not only more advanced experiences in writing skills but also an introduction to business studies, private correspondence, book-keeping and Civil Service Official Style Writing.

In 1870 the copy books took on an unprecedented dimension when Vere introduced a series of Drawing-Books designed to give pupils experience of technical skills. His advertisement stated:

> In order to elicit Irish latent talent, to increase the National power of competing with other nations in the production of designs applicable to every branch of manufacture, to place the best procurable models for imitation within the reach of the humblest child, to multiply the power of obtaining remunerative employment, and to furnish a fruitful source of useful instruction and innocent recreation, I have published a series of Elementary Drawing-Books especially adapted for special instruction in schools which have not the advantage of a drawing-master. No effort shall be wanting, and no expense spared to render the series both attractive and useful.[4]

The first Drawing Copy books became available almost immediately. Titles included 'Drawing to Scale', 'Architecture', 'Details of Tools',

'Workshop Drawings', 'Mechanics &c', 'The Human Figure in Outline' (14 in the series) and 'Ornamental Forms' (6 in the series). Later, he introduced Water Colour Copy Books containing simple painting lessons, landscapes and seascapes. Once again, as with his Copy Books, Vere paid considerable sums of money to leading educationalists and artists who assisted in their preparation. Thus, he paid the renowned artist, Sir Edward Poynter, £1,000 – a vast sum in Victorian times – for work on his Animal Studies series. Often the artistic details

ADVANCED STUDIES

OF

FLOWER PAINTING

IN WATER COLORS.

REPRODUCED FROM ORIGINAL DRAWINGS, SPECIALLY MADE FOR THE WORK

By ADA HANBURY

AND OTHER ARTISTS.

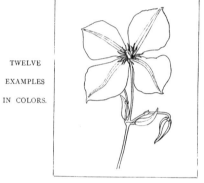

TWELVE

EXAMPLES

IN COLORS.

TWELVE

OUTLINES

IN PENCIL.

WITH FULL DIRECTIONS FOR COPYING THE EXAMPLES,
GENERAL INSTRUCTIONS ON PAINTING, AND A DESCRIPTION OF EACH FLOWER.

By BLANCHE HANBURY.

LONDON: BLACKIE & SON; GLASGOW, EDINBURGH, AND DUBLIN.
1885.

were the result of Foster's own suggestions; a notable example was his choice of an eight-year old Queen Victoria for the front cover of some of the earlier series. Surrounding this image were roses, shamrocks and thistles, along with drawings of children playing.

The entire expenditure on the Copy Books in their first seven years was approximately £50,000. The number of titles rose also to 192, becoming familiar sights in schools, not only throughout Ireland, but also in England, Wales, Scotland and the United States where the New

York Education Authority officially adopted them for its schools in 1871.

In their early years the printing and publishing of these series were handled by London and Dublin firms, but the quantity of orders soon became too great. Having decided he must streamline the operation, Vere transferred it entirely to an Irish firm, Marcus Ward & Co. of Belfast. He had earlier experienced the superior quality of their crafts-manship and had no doubts regarding their ability to cope with such a massive undertaking. The firm was delighted with the challenge and commenced the erection of new buildings and adoption of steam machinery at their Ulster Works at Marcus Ward Street, Belfast.

The choice of Marcus Ward & Co. marked the beginning of Vere Foster's long association with Belfast. Because he wished to be close to the production work, orders and correspondence, Vere moved to accommodation in the expanding industrial city. It was an attic in the house of Mrs Rodgers at 115 Great Victoria Street. For this he paid £1 weekly. This was now his only permanent address since his mother had died in London in 1867, leaving him no residence there.

Average annual book sales had now reached four million and his distributors were Whittaker & Co. of London and Marcus Ward & Co. of Belfast. Vere himself administered the entire order for copy books from the National Board of Education in Ireland. This considerable operation he carried out from the office which Marcus Ward had placed at his disposal in their building. Many teachers with whom he had correspondence had a great respect for Foster, remembering his earlier assistance. Once again, he was coming to their aid in ways they could never have imagined with his revolutionary copy books.

As mentioned, these became familiar in every vested and non-vested school in Ireland, something which did not go unnoticed by the school inspectorate. A typical report from one inspector in County Mayo in 1866 read:

... There is scarcely a school in the district of Westport in which these copy-books have not come into use during the year, and the teachers one and all appreciate them highly. In all good schools the whole of the Second Class now write paper (as opposed to slates) from Vere Foster's No 1 and No 2; the higher Classes using the more advanced Numbers of that excellent series ...[5]

As the number of titles grew, Vere kept nothing of the resulting huge profits for himself. There were three main beneficiaries:

The cause of Education in Ireland benefited greatly, particularly the hundreds of schools having insufficient deposits to obtain grants from the National Board. From the published list in his Belfast office in March 1879, these schools were chiefly in Counties Down, Tipperary, Meath, Cork, Fermanagh, Wicklow and Tyrone.

A second major beneficiary was Marcus Ward and Company for whom Vere paid the entire cost of the latest lithographic techniques which they were to use in his Water Colour copy books. Unfortunately the production costs of these new books were so heavy that Vere was forced to abandon temporarily his financial assistance to schools. (The new technology also resulted in Messrs Wards' machine-printing coloured Christmas cards and other water coloured publications. Vere was later to disclose that, for this work, Ward & Co. borrowed from him nearly all the capital he possessed though it was later repaid.)

Another important beneficiary from the sales of copy books was the Belfast Royal Hospital (now the Royal Victoria Hospital), on whose Board Foster served from 1875 until his death.

An exciting development took place in 1870. In that year, there commenced the 'Vere Foster National Competition in Writing, Lettering, Drawing and Painting'. Entries arrived in Belfast from schools all over Ireland and, gradually, from schoolchildren in Great Britain, the Cape of Good Hope, India, Jamaica, Newfoundland, Australia,

Constantinople and Burma. By 1898 Vere had awarded a total of 9,140 prizes from his now rapidly dwindling personal fortune. Prizewinners received 2s.6d. (half a crown) to £5 or Cards of Commendation.[6]

A selection of prizewinners he noted were Lizzie Farrelly, Hala Hhakalave, Mary Buggy, Andrew Hannay, Lily Hicks, Jose Guiliani, F W Hockley, John Burke, Inglis H Kilgaw, Chas E Scott, Frank Harcourt, Margaret Fleming, Haraki Haevalere and Edward E Stephens.[7] William H Spence, a pupil at Brown Street Male National School in Belfast, a short distance from Vere's address, won the First Prize of £5 for his entry in the Penmanship Section in June 1882 while Tom Ferguson from Cauvins Hospital, Portobello, Dublin was a First Prizewinner in August 1892. Both boys expressed their heartfelt thanks to Vere:

(27th June 1882) Brown Street Male National School, Belfast.
Vere Foster, Esq,

Dear Sir,
I beg to acknowledge with sincere gratitude your kind letter and gen-erous enclosure of £5 (First Prize) which you have awarded me in your Annual Competition in Penmanship. Your gift is greatly enhanced by the feeling that my perseverance has merited your high approval.

I am Sir, Your obedient Servant,
William H. Spence.[8]

Cauvins Hospital, Portobello, Dublin. Sept 4, 1892

Sir, Be pleased to accept my best thanks for the honour you have conferred me in awarding me the First Prize in the Original and Palmerston Series in your National Competition.

Your Obedient Servant, Tom Ferguson.[9]

To Vere Foster Esq᷑ from the children attending Killycarvan N. S. Co. Monaghan, Ireland.

We pupils so happy our schoolroom so neat,
Our floor is now boarded, it looks so complete;
Do thank most sincerely that man of great fame,
That lover of science Vere Foster by name.
For his princely donation unsolicited given,
We only can thank his Reward is in heaven.

And may heaven reward him with blessings Divine,
On earth to be happy in Glory to shine;
Is the wish and the prayer of each child in our isle,
Enjoying such comfort how happy they smile,
And sing – For his princely donation unasked for & given,
We only can thank – his reward is in heaven.

To the emigrant lonely he has been a guide,
To watch o'er the poor is his pleasure and pride,
To aid, to improve and to better their lot,
Abroad, on the ocean, or at home in their cot,
His princely donation so freely he's given,
We only can thank – his Reward is in heaven.

Should the great of our isle his example pursue,
How happy the land, Oh! what good they might do,
From the peer to the peasant, without regal rod,
All serving their country and loving their God,
For his princely donation unsolicited given,
We only can thank – his reward is in heaven.
      P.S. I rec᷑ the 2᷑ half note of your donation yesterday
            Yours very sincerely
                  Mic᷑ Connolly,
            Killycarvan. Jan᷑ 24ᵗʰ 1861.

To
Vere Foster Esq——

A poem from the children at Killycarvan school in County Monaghan.

Interesting, too, are the requests from the executives of two major banks in Belfast to have their staff improve their writing standards. The following letter must have given the philanthropist particular encouragement:

102 Great Brunswick St.
Dublin
25 October 1894

Vere Foster Esq.

Dear Sir,
On my return to the dear Old Land from a prolonged stay of years in the United States, I would like to have the pleasure of meeting you to talk with the man whom, from boyhood days, I do vividly recollect in connexion with Copy Books in School.

By the thousands and thousands of pounds which you have freely given all over the land as a stimulus to Good Penmanship, you must have done an immense service in the promotion of a branch of Education which I fear is often too much neglected even among the educated classes and the importance of which is not sufficiently recognised.

I remain, Faithfully Yours,
Henry Murphy.

The huge sales of Copy Books in every corner of the globe did not prevent differences and jealousies arising among the Ward brothers in their printing works. In 1876 John, one of the three brothers, decided to retire from the company and set up his own printing firm. Vere understood this desire and agreed with it. His decision, however, resulted in lengthy court proceedings which Vere had to attend.

John was successful but his two brothers claimed the lithographic stones for the Copy Books. In a further court action, Foster and John Ward appealed for their return. They were again successful when it was proved that the stones had been wilfully defaced by Marcus Ward. Vere was awarded £700 with costs. It was money and publicity he did not want, however.

The entire episode caused Vere to lose much of his interest in the production of his now world-famous Copy Books. As a result, he informed John Ward that because of what had happened and as he had achieved his original purpose of making his publications a success, he was going to retire from the enterprise. He offered to dispose of the Copyright, Goodwill, Plates, Blocks, Original Manuscripts, Drawing and Paintings and the entire plant of all his published works for a mere £3,000 to John Ward. He would, however, continue to control the very successful National Competitions and prizes to children.

It was Vere's understanding that Ward would continue printing the Vere Foster Copy Books as they were. But this did not happen. John Ward, having accepted Vere's magnificent offer, sold the entire enterprise to Blackie & Son, a small printing company with works in Dublin. Blackies transferred the work there from Belfast and also made plans for some printing to be carried out in England. But Vere used his prerogative to prevent this happening on the grounds that it would result in unnecessary loss of employment for people in Ireland. As a result of his action, the Vere Foster Copy Books continued to be printed in Ireland.

Further upheavals, however, lay ahead. In 1910, ten years after Vere's death, responsibility for his Copy Books passed into the hands of Thomas Nelson and Sons Ltd in England and the Educational Company of Ireland. Both printers continued to produce the Copy Books but, gradually, the output diminished. Incredibly, at the centenary of his death, all 192 titles of the *Vere Foster's Writing and Drawing Copy Books* are completely out of print.

I now realise the great privilege it was for me to have been taught penmanship in my early years through the use of the small number of *Vere Foster's Writing and Drawing Copy Books* kept permanently in the two-roomed country school I attended in south Down. Even now at the centenary of his death it gives me pleasure to know a teacher who still uses some of Vere Foster's writing material with his classes.

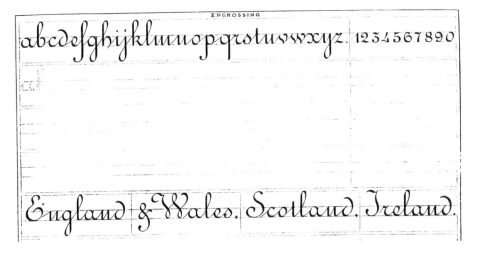

Copperplate writing excercises from a Copy book

Typical writing excercises in Vere Foster's Copy Books

TWELVE

TEACHERS'
CHAMPION

WHILE VERE WAS INVOLVED IN THE BUILDING and repair of schoolhouses and the production of Copy Books he was making yet another major contribution to education in Ireland. It was the improvement of the status of teachers. Being familiar with his work in this field, the National Association for the Promotion of Social Societies invited him to be guest speaker at their 1867 Annual Congress in Belfast.

In his speech Vere outlined the improvements in the conditions which, he believed, teachers were entitled to. These included:

i   an increase in salaries (at that time Irish National teachers were receiving only one third of those of elementary teachers in England and sometimes less than labourers' wages);

ii   teachers' salaries to be paid monthly, not quarterly;

iii the provision of rent-free houses – their building and upkeep to be paid out of public money. These would replace the numerous rented thatched cabins, especially in the Provinces of Ulster and Connacht;

iv   teachers to receive pensions on retirement (such were not generally available in those years);

v   a network of Union High Schools within walking distance for junior children, to serve as intermediate links between elementary schools and the various colleges;

vi   the establishment of many more Teachers' Associations, along with a teachers' journal, thus allowing all teachers to keep up to date with developments in their profession.

Within a few months this final suggestion was acted on with the publication of *The Irish Teachers' Journal* in January 1868. An unsigned letter in it was almost identical to the contents of Foster's earlier speech and was often attributed to him. The *Journal* later informed teachers who had begun meeting in groups or Teacher Associations that their Congress would be held on 15 August of that year in Denmark Street, Dublin. It did indeed take place and was to be the largest gathering of Irish teachers held up to that time.

Vere was invited to preside but could not accept as he was suffering from yet another attack of the *Washington* ophthalmia. However, he suggested that the post of president should be filled by a National School teacher rather than himself. A resolution 'that the thanks of this meeting are due, and are hereby tendered to (Vere Foster) for his able advocacy of our cause and for the kindly interest he has taken in our welfare' was carried by acclamation. After a full discussion during Congress, the title 'Irish National Teachers' Association' was chosen for the new national body and a paid secretary, Mr J Kavanagh was appointed.

Much work was left undone at that first meeting and it was arranged that a second Congress would be held on 29 and 30 December 1868. Vere was persuaded to become its first President and the very worthwhile event ended with a banquet in his honour.

As President of the INTA, Vere embarked on the huge amount of necessary work immediately. He spoke out trenchantly against the managerial system which deprived teachers of security of tenure for they were appointed without any definite system and dismissed without the right of appeal. His view that these functions should be carried out solely by school management committees did not endear him either to the Roman Catholic hierarchy or many senior Protestant clergy in Ulster. Besides being in favour of maintaining the status quo, these clerics were vehemently opposed to Vere's appeals for a higher guaranteed wage for teachers.

Vere's work with the Association was carried out alongside his other undertakings. These included the Copy Books, the school building repair and maintenance programme and his new 'East London Family Emigration Scheme'. During his first year as President of the Irish National Teachers' Association, Vere set up a committee comprising titled people and other persons of importance in London to help him with the assisted emigration of necessitous people from East London. It was a successful venture and resulted in several thousand emigrants leaving for Canada and Australia during the subsequent thirty years.

As Foster noted:

> The emigrants were selected without distinction of creed, from disadvantaged districts of the east of London by the clergy and others personally acquainted with them, and were people who, though of good character and ready and willing to work, were not able to in this country.[1]

A very happy relationship developed between Vere's East London Family Emigration Committee and the Canadian Government. Not only did the committee receive a letter of thanks from the Minister of Agriculture there for the highly suitable emigrants sent, but also Refund Bonuses (one such for £142.10s.) for those who had emigrated in 1872 and had resided in the Province of Ontario for three months.

Vere's work at the same time demanded that he travel abroad to study various aspects of education. He had in mind the welfare of teachers in Ireland and hoped to place them on a par with their peers in other countries. On one occasion in 1869 he decided to wait on the Lord Lieutenant, Earl Spencer, at the Viceregal Lodge in Phoenix Park, Dublin to lobby in favour of an Educational Rate to facilitate an increase in teachers' wages.

At about the same time he forwarded a petition to the Chief Secretary for Ireland, Chichester Fortesque, on behalf of a teacher in one of his brother's, Sir Cavendish's endowed schools near Ardee. Two years elapsed before Fortesque personally received a deputation led by Vere on the matter. In addition, the group presented a request, signed by 3,000 teachers, seeking an improvement in their conditions. This was met with outright rejection and a generally hostile attitude, illustrated by the Education Commission's decision to cut the grant to National schoolteachers towards the upkeep of their schoolhouses and the purchase of books. Teachers found the resultant financial hardship very difficult to cope with. An example from Belfast confirms this: in 1864, when No 2 North Queen Street was the town's Poor House, two of its inmates were William Vance, a schoolmaster and Miss M. Anderson, a schoolmistress.

Foster threw his unstinting support behind the teachers' cause and, as INTA President, attended many of their public meetings. He wrote letters of support to *The Irish Teachers' Journal*, to many Teachers' Associations and to the press. For four years his work for teachers was remorseless but he nevertheless felt an urge to resign to allow a member of the profession to become President. The Secretary of the Central Committee in Dublin, however, rejoined with an appeal to Vere 'to continue to occupy the position he has held ... From past experience they (the members) are convinced that Mr Foster's presence, advice and invaluable assistance are indispensable for the successful prosecution of their claims.'[2]

Remembered too was Vere's deputation of three teachers to the Liberal Prime Minister, William Gladstone himself, in February 1871 informing him of the needs of teachers in Ireland. The appreciation of the profession was eloquently recorded in *The Irish Teachers' Journal* of the same year:

> ... of the teachers' unreserved and indefatigable friend, Mr Vere Foster, we need say nothing. He has so thoroughly identified himself with the cause of his humbler countrymen that they look upon his co-operation as a matter of course. This, perhaps, is the best tribute we can pay to his active and untiring benevolence, though it may sometimes cause us to underrate, or rather not to perceive in a proper light, the real value of the services he has rendered to Irish education.

Vere acceded to the teachers' request to remain as their president. As such, he welcomed teachers to their Congress in Dublin a few months later on 26 December 1872. A number of the delegates, however, voiced disapproval of some memorials he had drafted regarding the means by which teachers' salaries might be increased and his demand that the power of dismissal should be withdrawn from School Managers and given to School Boards. This latter proposal was particularly unpopular with the Catholic clergy, among whom Vere maintained many intimate and respected friends. Vere was characteristically conciliatory towards his critics: '... He was sorry if he should excite any unfriendly feelings ... He had said enough about this question, he had now done with it.'[3]

Another memorial reflected his belief in using local taxation to help improve teachers' salaries and make them more secure. This he later clarified in a letter to *The Northern Whig* on 29 November 1873:

> ... I think it should ever be borne in mind when making comparisons between the incomes of Irish and English teachers, that the sole reason for the enormous disproportion between them lies in the fact that two-thirds of the support of schools in England are derived from local contributions but only one-seventh part in Ireland. I cannot be content going on beating the wind and whining to Government for what I know to be perfectly hopeless, and I wish to see my countrymen more self-reliant ...

> Vere Foster

Towards the end of the 1872 Congress Foster absented himself to allow the elections of a President and Vice-President to take place for the coming year. One of a small vociferous group reminded all present of Vere's wish to retire and added that there were plenty of men at the Congress, or of their own number, who were quite as competent to fill the position as Mr Foster. A motion was moved that a teacher should now be elected as President and this was passed, but not without disharmony. In the end, Vere Foster was asked to remain as Honorary President, to preside at the Congress and to appoint a Vice-President from among the members to preside on all occasions on which he could not attend.

But Vere suffered a further set-back before the conclusion of the Congress when an important memorial submitted by him for the welfare of teachers was rejected with applause by a 33 to 16 majority. When some senior members of the Association realised the enormity of their error they had the memorial slightly modified and distributed urgently by the Chief Secretary to all the Teachers' Associations. In a short time the modified memorial was approved and Vere continued as President.

While Vere continued to work tirelessly to improve the lot of Ireland's teachers, he did not neglect the maintenance and building of schoolhouses and the distribution of his Copy Books. As F. Frankfort Moore wrote in the *Belfast Tele*graph on 13 March 1924:

> Vere travelled throughout the country third class by rail and he denied himself an overcoat in the winter. He lived in the most meagre way, lodging in a single room – the 'bed-sitting room' of the lodging house and he used to send out his cheques from here with no fire in the grate.

Foster's greatest joy in these years was in awarding schoolchildren prizes in his 'Writing, Lettering, Drawing and Painting Competitions'. He was revered by teachers and the poor throughout Ireland while his journeyings brought him into contact with the relatives of folk whose emigration he had earlier arranged.

In 1873, he accepted an invitation from the Dublin Teachers' Association to address them later that year. A meeting took place in November 1873 in the Exhibition Room of the Rotunda, Dublin; the Lord Mayor was chairman, lending weight to their call for improved conditions.

Vere addressed the one thousand teachers present with vigour, again advocating the use of local taxation, combined with government funding, as a means of increasing their meagre salaries. Though heartened by the attendant publicity, Vere now knew there was nothing more he could do. He felt it imperative that he should step down at last from his privileged position of President of the National Teachers' Association and announced his decision in a letter to *The Irish Teachers' Journal*. In this, he stated 'that his resignation was necessary as his advocacy of local taxation and the necessary concomitant – school boards – might prove an embarrassment to the teachers' organisations'. It is clear also that his views had made him unpopular with a section of Belfast teachers at this time. Apart from his strong views on the control and management of schools, he was vehemently opposed to the 'Payment by Results' scheme on the grounds that it 'encouraged mediocrity and discouraged excellence'.[4]

Vere's resignation was a cause of great regret to an overwhelming majority of teachers. From across Ireland they wrote to the offices of *The Irish Teachers' Journal* and to his little attic room in Great Victoria Street, Belfast, many also remembering in their letters his generous gifts to them and provision of schoolhouses.

None of the Irish newspapers, including those in Belfast, could allow the 1873 Congress, Vere Foster's last as President, go unnoticed. On 31 December, *The Belfast Newsletter* mused:

> The reader will ask with surprise how men of education can be induced to work of drudgery for £15 a-year, or less than a shilling for the working day? … The teachers urge, therefore, that the minimum salaries should be raised to £52 a-year for men and £40 a-year for women … and that residences should be attached to the school-houses, teachers not having to find lodgings out of the wretched pittance allowed them and often two or three miles from the school …

At the conclusion of the 1873 Congress, a Mr Boal of the Belfast Teachers' Association was easily elected President of the INTA for the following year, thus breaking the control which Dublin had exercised over the Association.

In November 1873, the Belfast National Teachers' Association held a special public meeting similar to that of the Dublin Association four weeks previously. The aim of the Belfast gathering was to examine a paper by R.M. Chamney, a leading educationalist, published in *The Irish Teachers' Journal* regarding teachers' salaries. After some debate, Mr Boal took the chair. On the platform were the Mayor of Belfast, who presided, and other prominent dignitaries. Each in turn was requested by Boal to state his opinions on the matter. Vere Foster's opinions were not sought as he had not been invited to the meeting. Undaunted by this studied insult, however, he attended it, sitting unobtrusively among the body of the teachers present.

Yet, Foster was justifiably hurt by such calculated insolence to one who had sacrificed practically everything in the interests of education. In the wake of the Belfast meeting he sent a forthright letter to the *Northern Whig* and *The Irish Teachers' Journal*. In it he expressed a lively interest in the just agitation of the National Teachers for the redress of their many grievances and recalled the 'many practical proofs' of his sympathy for upwards of twenty years previous to the existence of any Teachers' Associations. He explained that the only reason for his not having taken part in the public meeting was because the Belfast Teachers' Association did not wish him to speak, or even take a place on the platform. In fact they had not even extended him the courtesy of inviting him to be present.

The Catholic and nationalist *Belfast Morning News* (later *The Irish News*) which often disagreed with Vere's stance on education in Ireland, in this instance voiced strong disapproval at his shabby treatment. The paper lamented that:

... one who in an especial sense has made himself the champion of the National Schoolteachers, should have been overlooked, in the manner he describes (in his letter) ... Mr Foster is kind enough to furnish them with an excuse, but it is scarcely one under which the officials can shield themselves ... [5]

If, on reflection, the Belfast Teachers' Association felt it had made a mistake in not inviting Foster to their Special Teachers' Meeting, an opportunity to make amends soon arose. On the following Saturday the BTA held their Annual Soiree in McQuiston's School-house in Donegall Pass, a few hundred yards from Vere's residence in Great Victoria Street, Belfast. But, once again, he was snubbed. It was normally a happy get-together which Vere had always attended. On this occasion, after tea had been served to the gathering in the lower school-rooms, the company moved to the upper school-room. There they listened to Mr Boal give a lengthy address on the December 1873 Congress in Dublin at which he was elected President. His colleague, a Mr Cullen gave a history of the BTA. Throughout the evening songs were sung by Miss Doyle, Miss Anderson and Miss Boal.

Vere was well aware of this sharp antagonism towards him by 'the Belfast men' but it did not cause him to lose interest in the welfare of their profession. Over twenty years later, in 1896, so much was he still loved and remembered by the general body of Irish teachers that he was invited to be an honoured guest and speaker at the Annual Congress of the Irish National Teachers' Association. Ironically, it was held in Belfast.

How happy the ageing philanthrophist must have been among the huge gathering at that Congress which he described as 'a non-political and non-sectarian body, composed of teachers of every denomination', which he had helped found.[6]

Vere's active work with teachers came to an end when he severed his connection with the INTA. It was then he embarked on other strenuous work which he felt was awaiting his attention.

No. 115 Great Victoria Street, Belfast (now demolished) was
Vere Foster's residence when he died in December 1900.

THIRTEEN

VERE'S
FINAL DAYS

ALMOST IMMEDIATELY VERE IMMERSED HIMSELF in various
aspects of life in Belfast. One, in particular, involved collecting
subscriptions from the local people for the upkeep of the Belfast Royal
Hospital. He was elected to the Board in 1875 and became a Life
Member in the following year. During that year he made 9,000 personal calls, besides posting a large number of circulars. But Vere was not

averse to more direct methods of fund-raising such as sitting on the pavement in Donegall Place in all weathers 'holding forth a plate to receive subscriptions'. On 21 August 1877 he wrote to A.J. Macrory, Hon Secretary, enclosing £524.10s.6d:

> ... With regard to next year's collection, I request the Board's permission to act as their Hon. Collector, in which case I will use my best exertions to obtain as large an increase of funds as possible, and will add 10 per cent to all new subscriptions under £1 which I may succeed in obtaining ...
>
> Yours sincerely
> Vere Foster

The hospital's Board of Management accepted this offer gratefully and in their Annual Report for 1878 it was noted that Mr Foster had kept his promise and that the total of the collection that year 'showed an increase of upwards of £200 on the collection of last year.'[1] The Belfast Royal Hospital further reaped the financial benefits of Foster's generosity as he donated to it at least half of his ongoing income from the sales of the Copy Books.

At that time the awful state of much of Belfast's housing caused Vere considerable heart-searching. Bye-laws designed to improve the situation had made little impact. In 1873, the Medical Officer at Ligoniel described many recently built one-storey mill-houses as not being fit shelter for domesticated animals, much less human beings. They had flat wooden roofs, the privy accommodation was public and abominable and the floors of the back rooms were usually saturated with sewage.

In the 1860s a group of public-spirited men had met to consider this question. Among them was the prominent local architect, Charles Sherry and together they worked assiduously to improve the town's housing. Vere joined the group. Sherry had plans drawn up for the improvement of working-class housing in Belfast, but unfortunately died before work was due to commence. Vere referred to this sad event in a letter to the *Belfast Morning News* of 14 April 1871:

> As he (Mr Sherry) had made it an object of special study to prepare plans of labourers' dwellings of suitable and economic construction ... I suggest that an appropriate form for the proposed tribute would be – first, to erect a monumental cross ... and ... to apply the surplus of such amount as might be raised by subscription, to the erection of a row of labourers' dwellings according to his own plans and to call them by his name ... I shall have much satisfaction in subscribing £100 ... as I believe 'they mourn the dead who do as they desire'.

The fact that Mr Sherry was a Roman Catholic was irrelevant to Foster. As Mary McNeill has observed: 'It is all perfectly in character – the overstepping of religious barriers, the sympathy with any plans to help the working man and the instant lavish generosity'.[2]

Vere became increasingly bound to the life of Belfast. Numerous charities, like the Belfast Nursing Society, were recipients of his aid. In the late 1870s, however, he found it difficult to maintain his financial help for the Royal Hospital as distress had returned again to the people of Ireland. Another failure of the potato crop resulted in starvation, cruelty and evictions by landlords, especially in the west. Death, political unrest and massive emigration were once again Ireland's lot. In response, Vere embarked on a second phase of his assisted emigration programme. He began by founding an 'Emigration Fund', soliciting donations through personal contact. One such request was an open letter to the Irish Home Rule leader, Charles Stewart Parnell, MP, then in the United States of America, collecting funds for relief of the distress in Ireland. It was printed in the *Northern Whig* on 10 January 1880. Foster made it clear that he was opposed both to Parnell's advice to the tenants not to pay exorbitant rents and the compulsory purchase of the landlords' estates by the government to enable the creation of a class of owner-occupiers. (This solution was finally adopted by the Wyndham Land Act of 1903).

> It is as natural for young people to emigrate from over-peopled countries to new regions as it is for young bees to swarm, and it is unstatesmanlike and cruel to the poor to contravene the laws of nature by decrying emigration as some people do. ... I took an active part in organising emigration from Ireland to America between twenty and thirty years ago ... I am now too old to resume the necessary labour ... you might be eminently successful in conferring lasting benefits on great numbers of poor people whose normal state is ever verging on starvation ... In proof of my sincerity I hereby subscribe £2 for each young man and woman between 18 and 35 years of age ... emigrants to be from the province of Connaught or from the counties of Donegal, Clare, Kerry or Cork ...

> I am, sir, your obedient servant,
> Vere Foster.

Belfast, January, 1880.

In a quite offensive reply to Vere and signed, 'Captain Rock, 2 November 1880', Parnell refused to have anything to do with his proposal and instead, led the Land League's campaign for radical land reform. Some Irish-Americans, such as the former Fenian and leading Boston editor, John Boyle O'Reilly, wrongly accused Foster of being implicated in a British plot to 'banish Irish people from Ireland'. Deeply hurt, Vere sought to 'persuade my friend O'Reilly that such a theory was arrant nonsense', but in vain.[3] His emigration scheme had, however, drawn support from the *New York Times* of 6 January 1881:

We have an abundance of fertile soil awaiting the hands of cultivators – far richer than any in Ireland – which can be bought for a great deal less money. We welcome the suffering Irish to this heritage, and will create a fund to defray the expenses of emigration ... This mode of relief for Ireland is both practical and legitimate, and we commend it to the consideration of Mr Parnell.

Despite Parnell's rejection, replies to Vere's open letter flooded in from many Protestants and Catholics, often supported by appeals from their respective churches.

It is estimated that during the following twenty years, Foster helped a total of 25,000 emigrants, mostly females, to travel to the United States. The procedure for emigration followed the earlier pattern, while he particularly assisted emigrants from the west of Ireland, again 'loaning them' their fares. Once he had satisfied himself as to their character, Vere arranged for employers in America to receive them on arrival; others had relations already there. Sometimes he was forced to encourage females to have their brothers travel with them on their sea journeys, or he travelled with them himself.

The constant requests from emigrants for assistance seriously depleted his personal financial assets and he was forced to call on politicians and prominent individuals for help. He was not always successful with his requests but several wealthy individuals provided subscriptions of as much as £100 or £200 monthly. Among these were Charles Wilson of Cheltenham and William Moore of London.[4] The fifth Earl Spencer, Lord Lieutenant of Ireland under Gladstone, also enclosed a subscription, explaining that while he would prefer to see reform, he admired Foster's efforts.[5] However, Miss Knollys, writing on behalf of Her Royal Highness, the Princess of Wales, declined; the reason given to Vere was the excessive number of requests reaching HRH.[6]

Though concerned solely with the welfare of the Irish people, Foster did have views on the great political questions of the day. A Liberal who admired Gladstone's 'great genius and many noble qualities', he remained opposed to the Prime Minister's Irish Land Act of 1881 and his Home Rule Bill of 1886. Vere was firmly opposed to state purchase of landed estates as 'the public robbery of one class ... for the benefit of another'. Instead, he favoured the break-up of estates through the modification of the law of inheritance to divide the property of deceased persons equally among the next of kin. This, he felt, would bring about a peaceful reform of the land system in Ireland.

In a letter to Gladstone, dated 24 February 1886, Vere warned of Ulster Protestant opposition to Home Rule and expressed his fear that the scheme might result in 'a bloody Civil War between different portions of the Irish people and between Great Britain and Ireland'. As one who had had long denounced British misrule in Ireland, Vere felt that Ireland's best hope lay not in separation, but in a 'more perfect union' between the two countries. A pacifist, he once wrote that, 'I cannot bring myself to approve of the shedding of human blood for any purpose, however righteous'. Yet, his views remained fluid on the Irish Question and, writing to Lady Aberdeen in August 1886, after the defeat of Gladstone's Home Rule Bill, he suggested that the best solution might lie in a scheme of devolution for the United Kingdom with 'the establishment of four provincial parliaments in Ireland'.[7]

In a sense, Vere's political views were neither narrowly nationalist nor narrowly unionist. They were informed by his deep humanitarianism and so were unique in the context of the struggle over Home Rule in late nineteenth century Ireland.

In religious affairs, Foster was a strong advocate of complete religious equality. Though an Anglican, he was totally ecumenical in his outlook. He strongly opposed the privileged position of the Church of Ireland up to 1869, declaring at a Liberal meeting in County Louth in 1865:

He did not want any ascendancy at all but equality, and if they had

112

that, there would be a great deal more union of persons of all denominations for the common good. He thought a Catholic as good as a Protestant and a Protestant as good as a Catholic ...[8]

Vere Foster in middle age

FOURTEEN

A LIFE OF UNCEASING DEVOTION
TO HUMANITY

THE END, FOR VERE, came as unostentatiously as he had lived, in cheap attic lodgings at 115, Great Victoria Street, after a long period of indifferent health, on 21 December 1900. The tragic circumstances of his death were poignantly described by the artist and engraver, John Vinycomb in a letter to the Belfast antiquarian, FJ Bigger on the following day: '... So dear old Mr Foster is gone ... Bernard called yesterday to see him but found only his poor remains.

Grand old man!'[1] At his funeral to the City Cemetery there was a mere handful of mourners, a tribute perhaps to the unobtrusive way he had carried out his philanthropic work. On that occasion, it was well said:

> He had the spirit of the true and gentle knight. He knew how to do great things simply. He was full of high-bred chivalry towards the ignorant and the poor. He gave everything to them and it made him happy to take Poverty as his bride for the good of man … the age of heroes and saints is not only in the past.

Belfast's two morning papers were fulsome in their tributes, thus dispelling any previous ambiguities in their assessments of Vere's manifold activities. The *Belfast Newsletter* of Saturday, December 22, 1900, recorded its appreciation in these terms:

> It will generally be recognised that in him there has passed away a citizen who … 'loved his fellow men' … and all who honour true goodness and nobility of character will mourn his loss as that of a friend and benefactor … It can safely be predicted that the good deeds of the philanthropist … will long be revered as that of a man whose life story is a record of unselfish devotion to the cause of humanity.

The *Irish News and Belfast Morning News* of the same date observed:

> The death of Mr Vere Foster (yesterday) severs one of those links which connect the present with the past. For many years, Mr Foster had been prominently identified with works of charity and benevolence and numerous were those who felt the kindness of his heart. Selfishness was unknown in his character. Zeal and philanthropy were characteristic of him and to such an extent did his fellows lead him that his financial resources were taxed to a great extent. In these circumstances, it was but natural that the regret experienced on his death should be widespread.

Of Vere's declining years we know little. Having been under the care of Dr Victor Fielden with occasional visits from Professor William Whitla, MD for a year prior to his death, he had nonetheless been confined to the house for not more than six or seven weeks. He therefore retained his faculties to a remarkable degree, even sending his usual annual subscription in September of £5 to the Belfast Day Nurseries with an accompanying letter expressing his approval of the way in which the work was being carried on. Also, we know of his 1897 publication of a book entitled *The Two Duchesses*. This comprises correspondence between two Duchesses of Devonshire, the Earl of Bristol (Vere's paternal great-grandfather) and other eminent persons, relating chiefly to events between the years 1777 and 1859. It was a remarkable achievement for a man of almost eighty years of age.

We have already mentioned his sterling efforts on behalf of the Royal Hospital where his personal canvassing raised a larger sum for the institution than had ever been subscribed in any previous year. He was also one of the original promoters of the Belfast School of Art and, in addition to a donation of £20 and an annual subscription, he personally guaranteed the Headmaster's salary for a number of years. Apart from this, he bore the expense of putting several young students through Queen's College, now Queen's University, Belfast. In his position of first President of what became the INTO (Irish National Teachers' Organisation), he spoke against the 'invidious' Payment by Results system at its Congress in Belfast at Easter, 1896.[2]

It is touching that for his last seven or eight months, Vere was accompanied by Miss Mary Anne Foster, his grand-niece, who attended him in his illness. This lady was later well known as 'Aunt Anna' on *Radio Eireann* and also for her contributions on Greek and Irish mythology on BBC Radio's 'Children's Hour'. Due to her very poor eyesight, she was knocked down twice in Belfast and repaid the Mater Infirmorum and City Hospitals by going to each, once a week, to read to sick children.

One of his closest friends, in what must be a conservative estimate, stated that Vere Foster must have spent over £120,000 during his long life in the cause of charity. Because he was never married and his mode of living was one of the simplest, he eschewed the luxuries of life in order that he might spend his money in doing good. Indeed, all found in him a stimulating companion, for he was a man of culture, refinement and wide experience. He had seen life in many parts of the world and his unfailing courtesy in his relationships, coupled with his total dedication to the poor, meant that, for him, the concept of the 'brotherhood of man' was not an empty phrase, but a principle by which he lived and died.

Vere Foster's grave in Belfast City Cemetery

EPILOGUE

A T THIS POINT IN THE NARRATIVE, literally in its closing para-
graph, the author became seriously ill, requiring hospitalisation
and he died peacefully on 5 September, 1999. It seemed fitting to his
family and his close circle of friends, many of whom had assisted him
in the production of the text, that this small volume be published.

It stands as a tribute not only to the diligent research of Brendan
Colgan, but much more, (and this he would have wished), to the glori-
ous memory of Vere Louis Henry Foster, who became for Brendan and
many others a fountain of inspiration, a true educationalist and lover of
the poor, a true nobleman whose breadth of vision enabled him to cross

boundaries of class, culture and creed for the sake of the progress of the people of Ireland – a message we surely need as we enter a new Millennium.

Accordingly, the family and friends of the author wish to thank all those who in any way have made possible the publication of this volume. May the light which Vere Foster shone on his contemporaries continue to point to new possibilities of service and reconciliation in our divided land.

SELECT
BIBLIOGRAPHY

PRIMARY SOURCES

Public Record Office of Northern Ireland: Foster of Glyde Papers, D.3618.
Belfast Central Library: F.J. Bigger Papers.

OFFICIAL PUBLICATIONS

Report of Select Committee on Passengers' Act, 1851.
Annual Reports of Commissioners of National Education in Ireland.

NEWSPAPERS AND PERIODICALS

Belfast Evening Telegraph
Belfast Morning News
Irish Farmers' Gazette, 1851–52
Irish News
Irish Teachers' Journal, 1868–72
Northern Whig
The Belfast News-Letter
The Freeman's Journal
The Irish Times
The Times

SECONDARY SOURCES

ALLISON, R.S., *The Seeds of Time, Being a Short History of the Belfast General and Royal Hospital 1850-1903*, Belfast, 1972.

BALL, T.H., 'The Famine – Its Cause and Cure. A Sermon preached in the Parish Church of Mullabrack, Diocese of Armagh, on 24 March, 1847 by Rev Thomas Hanley Ball, A.B.', Dublin, Samuel B. Oldham, 1847.

BATTRICK, JACK, *Brownsea Islander*, as told by Gail Lawson, Poole Historical Trust, 1978.

BENCE-JONES, MARK, *Burke's Guide to Country Houses: vol. 1: Ireland*, London, 1978

CARDWELL, E, KELLY, V AND MAGOWAN, S., *Emigration in Victorian Times*, Stranmillis College, 1994.

DOWLING, P.J., *The Hedge Schools of Ireland*, Mercier Press, 1968.

FOSTER, VERE, *Origin and History of Vere Foster's Writing and Drawing Copy Books*, 1882.

FOSTER, VERE (editor), *The Two Duchesses*, Blackie & Sons, London, 1898.

GARNER, EDWARD, *To Die by Inches. The Famine in North East Cork*, Midleton, Co Cork, 1986.

HANBURY, ADA, *Vere Foster's Drawing Books: Advanced Studies of Flower Painting in Water Colours*, London, Blackie & Son, 1885.

HICKEY, D.J. and DOHERTY, J.E., *A Dictionary of Irish History Since 1800*, Dublin, 1980.

KILLEN, JOHN (editor), *The Famine Decade. Contemporary Accounts 1841–1851*, Blackstaff Press, 1995.

LEGG, RODNEY, *Brownsea – Dorset's Fantasy Island*, Yeovil, 1986.

McCUNE REID, H.F., *A Short Biographical Study of Vere Foster, First President*, Irish National Teachers' Organisation Bangor Congress Committee, 1956.

McNEILL, MARY, *Vere Foster 1819–1900. An Irish Benefactor*, David and Charles, Newton Abbott, 1970.

NEWMAN, KATE, *Dictionary of Ulster Biography*, Belfast, 1993.

O'CONNELL, T.J., *A History of the Irish National Teachers' Organisation, 1868-1968*, Dublin, 1968.

PHOENIX EAMON (editor), *A Century of Northern Life: The Irish News and 100 Years of Ulster History 1890s–1990s*, Belfast, 1995.

SHANNON MILLIN, S., *Sidelights on Belfast History*, Belfast and London, 1932.

TUKE, JAMES, *A Visit to Connaught in 1847*, London, 1847.

WOODHAM-SMITH, CECIL, *The Great Hunger*, London, 1962.

NOTES

ONE pp1–6

1 Rodney Legg, Brownsea: *Dorset's Fantasy Island*, Dorset Publishing Company, p.16.
2 Jack Battrick, *Brownsea Islander*, Poole Historical Trust, 1978, p.11.
3 H.F. McCune Reid, *A Short Biographical Study of Vere Foster, First President*, (I.N.T.O. Bangor Congress Committee, 1956), pp.1–2.

TWO pp7–14

1 *The Vindicator*, Belfast, 22 October 1845
2 *The Illustrated London News* (hereafter I.L.N.), 29 August 1846
3 *Times*, 16 April 1847
4 ibid, 24 March 1847
5 M. Bence-Jones, *Burke's Guide to Country Houses, vol 1, Ireland*, London, 1978, p.141; Buildings of Architectural Interest in County Louth, p.86.

THREE pp15–20

1 *The Liverpool Albion*, 16 May 1850.
2 D. Hollett, *Passage to the New World, Passage Ships and Irish Famine Emigrants 1845–1952*, Abelgenny, 1995 (hereafter P.N.W.), p.69.
3 Stanley Hyland, *Curiosities from Parliament (Three Ships' Doctors)*, p.115.
4 Vere Foster, *Work and Wages or The Penny Emigrant's Guide to the United States and Canada* (London, 1852).

FOUR pp21–27

1 *I.L.N.*, 13 February 1848.
2 PRONI, D. 3618/C/45.
3 Killen, John (ed.), *The Famine Decade Contemporary Accounts 1841–1851*, The Blackstaff Press, 1995, p.8.
4 *I.L.N.*, 3 August 1849.

FIVE pp28–35

1 Killen, John, *The Famine Decade*: The Blackstaff Press, p.83.
2 Augustus Foster's Diary, 30 December 1847.
3 *The Vindicator*, 23 December 1846.

4 Tuke, James H., *A Visit to Connaught in Autumn of 1847*, London, 1847, p.19.
5 Hyland, Stanley, *Curiosities from Parliament*, 1856, p.121.
6 Tuke, James H., *A Visit to Connaught in Autumn of 1847*, p.17; *An extract from an address to the Lord Lieutenant of Ireland*, signed by the Relief Committee of Swinford Union, County Mayo, 1846.

SIX pp36–40

1 *R.N. Education in Ireland*, 1850, p.264.
2 'Broadsheet on Emigration', cited in Mary McNeill, *Vere Foster*, Newton Abbot, 1971, p.57.
3 M.A. Busteed, *Irish Emigration Documents*, p.150.
4 *The Non-Subscribing Presbyterian Magazine*, 1943, p.65.

SEVEN pp41–50

1 Hyland, Stanley, *Curiosities from Parliament*, London, 1856, p.121.
2 ibid., p.112
3 ibid., p.113
4 ibid., p.113
5 ibid., p.112
6 ibid., p.112
7 House of Commons Blue Book (Parliamentary Papers No 40), 1851
8 Laxton, Edward, *The Famine Ships*, p.201.

EIGHT pp51–56

1 *Irish Farmers' Gazette*, 1852
2 *The Belfast Newsletter*, 22 December, 1900
3 PRONI, D.3618/D/31
4 Percival, John, *The Great Famine*, p.133
5 *Irish Farmers' Gazette*, 1852.

NINE pp57–70

1 Laxton, Edward, *The Famine Ships, the Irish Exodus to America*, p.201.
2 *Belfast Newsletter*, 22 December, 1900.
3 McNeill, Mary, *Vere Foster*, p.83.
4 PRONI, D.3618/D.10/4-5.
5 PRONI, D.3618/D/6/126
6 PRONI, D.3618/D/3/2
7 PRONI, D.3618/D/5/5
8 PRONI, D.3618/D/3/2; H.F. McCune Reid, *A Short Biographical Study of Vere Foster*, pp.5–6.

9   Vere Foster to Cavendish Foster, 6 April 1858, cited in Mary McNeill, *Vere Foster*, pp.98–99.

10 Letter from Vere Foster, 23 April 1856, cited in McNeill, op.cit., pp.89–90.

11 Vere Foster's lecture: 'From Belfast to Pile of bones and the End of the Track' – given in the Rosemary Street Hall, Belfast on 22 January 1883.

12 Ibid.

TEN pp71–80

1   Dowling, P.J., *The Hedge Schools of Ireland*, Mercier, 1968, p.36; *Famous Maghera Men*, Belfast, n.d., pp.40–41.

2   Hickey, D.J. and Doherty, J.E., *A Dictionary of Irish History Since 1800* (Dublin, 1980), pp.386-8; Rafferty, Oliver P., *Catholicism in Ulster: An Interpretative History* (Dublin, 1994), pp.114–122.

3   *R.N. Educ.*, 1863, p.231

4   Minutes of National Board of Education, 4.2.1859

5   PRONI, D.3618/E/1/1-4

6   ibid.

7   ibid.

8   *R.N. Educ*, 1859, p.251

9   ibid., p.222

ELEVEN pp81–95

1   Gray, Peter, *The Irish Famine*, New Horizons, p.151

2   ibid., p.150

3   Foster, Vere, *Origin and History of Vere Foster Writing and Drawing Copy Books*

4   McCune Reid, H.F., *A short Biographical Study of Vere Foster*, p.14.

5   *R.N. Education*, 1866, p.225

6   PRONI, D.3618/E/5/5

7   ibid

8   PRONI, D.3618/E/5/11

9   PRONI, D.3618/E/3/21

TWELVE pp96–106

1   Foster, Vere, *East London Family Emigration Fund*, p.2

2   *Irish Teachers' Journal*, 1873, p.483

3   ibid., p.5

4   McCune Reid, H.F., *Vere Foster*, pp.17–18.

5   *Belfast Morning News*, from Irish Teachers' Journal, 1874, p.117

6   *Irish Teachers' Journal*, 1874, p.9

THIRTEEN pp107–113

1   Allison, R.S., *The Seeds of Time – A Short History of the Belfast General and Royal Hospital, 1850–1903*, Belfast, 1972, pp.100–102.
2   McNeill, Mary, *Vere Foster 1819–1900: An Irish Benefactor* (Newton Abbot, 1970), pp.138–9.
3   PRONI, op.cit., pp.196–7.
4   PRONI, D.3618/D/22/5.
5   PRONI, D.3618/D/22/39.
6   PRONI, D.3618/D/28/4–12.
7   McNeill, op.cit., pp.199–200
8   *Irish Times*, 19 June 1865.

FOURTEEN pp114–117

1   Vinycomb, J. to F.J. Bigger, 21 December 1900, (Belfast Central Library, F.J Bigger Collection, J Vinycomb Letters, 61).
2   McCune Reid, H.F., *A Short Biographical Study of Vere Foster, First President*, p.18.